P9-DBK-536

DIABETIC LIVING Holiday COOKING VOLUME 8

DIABETIC LIVING® HOLIDAY COOKING
IS PART OF A BOOK SERIES PUBLISHED BY
BETTER HOMES AND GARDENS SPECIAL
INTEREST MEDIA, DES MOINES, IOWA

Rosemary Roasted
Chicken with
Tangerine-Walnut
Bulgur Pilaf
recipe, p. 70

From the Editors

Holiday time brings families home and friends together for gatherings that always involve food. Sharing meals and celebrating doesn't mean your daily dietary plan gets pushed to the side, however. This collection of holiday recipes will help you enjoy the best of the season and feel good.

Impress your guests with special breakfast dishes, holiday breads, mouthwatering main dishes, and spectacular desserts. You'll also find simpler fare for busy weekdays and last-minute revelers. Each recipe has been thoroughly tested in the Better Homes and Gardens® Diabetic Living® Test Kitchen for accuracy, ease of preparation, and great taste. The recipes include complete nutrition information so you can track calories, carbs, fat, and sodium to make sure you are meeting your meal-plan goals.

Stay ahead of holiday stress with our helpful management tips. Look for stress-busting suggestions, time-savers, and ideas for avoiding holiday weight gain. When the holidays arrive, you'll be relaxed and ready with a plan for great food and good fun.

31

69

On the Cover:

Chocolate-Cranberry Cake with Almond Filling
recipe, *p. 149*

Photographer: Jason Donnelly
Food Stylist: Dianna Nolin

116

EDITORIAL ADVISORY BOARD

The following experts review articles that appear in *Diabetic Living®* magazine:

Sheri R. Colberg, Ph.D., FACSM, professor emerita of exercise science at Old Dominion University; 2016 ADA Outstanding Diabetes Educator

Marjorie Cypress, Ph.D., CNP, CDE, Albuquerque-based consultant; past president of health care and education, ADA

Joanne Gallivan, M.S., RDN, National Diabetes Education Program director at the NIH

Sharonne N. Hayes, M.D., FACC, FAHA, cardiologist and founder of the Women's Heart Clinic at Mayo Clinic

Manny Hernandez, Diabetes Hands Foundation cofounder; executive at Livongo Health

Marty Irons, RPh, CDE, community pharmacist, author; served in industry and military

Francine R. Kaufman, M.D., chief medical officer and vice president of Global Medical Affairs at Medtronic Diabetes

Nathan A. Painter, Pharm.D., CDE, associate clinical professor at UC San Diego Skaggs School of Pharmacy

Chef Art Smith, Florida-based star of Bravo's *Top Chef Masters* and former personal chef for Oprah Winfrey

Hope S. Warshaw, M.M.Sc., RD, CDE, author of *Diabetes Meal Planning Made Easy* and *Eat Out, Eat Well,* published by the ADA

John Zrebiec, M.S.W., CDE, director of Behavioral Health Services at the Joslin Diabetes Center and lecturer in psychiatry at Harvard Medical School

GUIDE TO CREDENTIALS:
CDE: Diabetes educator, **CNP:** Nurse practitioner, **FACC:** American College of Cardiology fellow, **FACSM:** American College of Sports Medicine fellow, **FAHA:** American Heart Association fellow, **M.D.:** Doctor of Medicine, **M.M.Sc.:** Master of Medical Science, **M.S.:** Master of Science, **M.S.W.:** Master of Social Work, **RD:** Dietitian, **RDN:** Dietitian nutritionist, **Pharm.D.:** Doctor of Pharmacy, **Ph.D.:** Doctor of Philosophy, **RPh:** pharmacist

Holiday COOKING VOLUME 8

CONSUMER MARKETING

Vice President, Consumer Marketing	STEVE CROWE
Consumer Marketing Product Director	HEATHER SORENSEN
Consumer Marketing Billing/Renewal Manager	TAMI PERKINS
Consumer Marketing Product Manager	WENDY MERICAL
Business Director	DIANE UMLAND
Production Manager	AL RODRUCK
Contributing Project Manager	SHELLI MCCONNELL, PURPLE PEAR PUBLISHING, INC.
Contributing Photographer	JASON DONNELLY
Contributing Food Stylist	DIANNA NOLIN
Test Kitchen Director	LYNN BLANCHARD
Test Kitchen Chef	CARLA CHRISTIAN, RD, LD

DIABETIC LIVING® MAGAZINE

Editorial Director	JENNIFER DARLING
Executive Editor	JENNIFER WILSON
Creative Director	MICHAEL BELKNAP
Senior Associate Editor	CAITLYN DIIMIG, RD
Associate Editor	BAILEY MCGRATH
Art Director	NIKKI SANDERS
Art Director	DEB BERGER
Administrative Assistant	LORI EGGERS

MEREDITH NATIONAL MEDIA GROUP

President JON WERTHER

Chairman and Chief Executive Officer STEPHEN M. LACY

Vice Chairman MELL MEREDITH FRAZIER

In Memoriam— E.T. MEREDITH III (1933–2003)

Diabetic Living® Everyday Cooking is part of a series published by Meredith Corp., 1716 Locust St., Des Moines, IA 50309-3023.

If you have comments or questions about the editorial material in *Diabetic Living® Holiday Cooking,* write to the editor of *Diabetic Living* magazine, Meredith Corp., 1716 Locust St., Des Moines, IA 50309-3023. Send an e-mail to *diabeticlivingmeredith.com* or call 800/678-2651.
Diabetic Living® magazine is available by subscription or on the newsstand. To order a subscription to the magazine, go to *DiabeticLivingOnline.com*

© Meredith Corporation 2017. All rights reserved.

First edition. Printed in U.S.A.

ISSN 1943-2887   ISBN 978-0696-30265-7

CONTENTS

Help!
IT'S THE HOLIDAYS

This time of year is full of family gatherings, sweet festivities, and treasured traditions—plus the challenge of preparing for it all. Maybe you're also missing lost loved ones or dealing with a family problem—the stuff of life that can go hand in hand with the holidays.

It's easy to push your health aside with all of the activities. But don't. You can't control everything. You can, however, pay attention to yourself and still manage the highs and lows of the season as well as your glucose levels.

Learn some new strategies to use this season. They will help reduce stress (which allows you to control your blood sugar), keep weight gain in check (even with all the holiday spreads), and show you ways to work ahead so the big gathering doesn't fill you with anxiety.

Start by slowing down for a minute. Take a deep breath, pull up a chair, relax, and read on.

Stress

Long-term stress levels increase blood glucose levels—so taming the seasonal stress monster is essential for managing diabetes. Some tips to help:

Play It Steady. Do your best to stick with your medication, food, and exercise schedules. For most people, the holidays are a wonderful time of year, but they can mean additional pressures when you have diabetes. So schedule some time every day to use usual methods for yourself to relax and decompress.

Designate Elves. Don't overload yourself with work—delegate tasks and chores. You don't have to—and you shouldn't—do everything alone. Gathering together is one of the best parts of the holidays, so recruit one of your guests, friends, or a family member to join you in the kitchen. Ask someone to set the table and others to clean up. Consider hosting a potluck instead of cooking an entire meal alone. It's more fun, too.

Go Solo. If you think you'll need a break and you can afford it, consider staying at a hotel while visiting family. Though family members might try to persuade you to stay with them, ask yourself if this is in their best interest or yours. Sleeping in a hotel bed can be nicer than a pullout couch in the middle of a living room.

Treat Yourself. Remember to treat yourself gently. Play music or book a massage. Get enough sleep each night or take a power nap—it wards off irritability and mood swings.

If it helps, grab your journal and take note of the highs and lows, as well as what you're thankful for.

Keep the Peace. Meditation and breath work may relax you. Try closing your eyes and counting 100 breaths or just sit quietly and repeat a thought that calms you.

If there's a family squabble, remember: Most people don't deliberately try to upset others. If the relatives are good listeners, tell them you're upset with an "I feel ____ when you ____" statement. In the end, you may have to limit contact with some individuals. Cultivating relationships that are positive is mutually rewarding.

You always have the choice to allow someone to upset you or to let the matter drop.

Exercise. Exercise reduces stress and helps to control glucose levels, so keep moving this season. Try home exercise videos or walking. Or start a holiday tradition that gets everyone moving. Suggest a game of touch football or sign up for a turkey trot on Thanksgiving morning.

At minimum, stretch often. It helps keep you mindful of your body and your feelings.

AVOID THE HOT ZONE

Holiday revelers need to be aware of the "Hot Zone"–a family gathering, a company party, or any event that involves food and drink.

Devise a plan for your situation. Maybe you choose to eat what others are eating, but in small quantities, Or you make a point to grab a healthy snack prior so you stay satisfied through hors d'oeuvre hour—think low-fat yogurt or cheese, half of a whole grain granola bar, or a handful of nuts.

The social pressure to eat at parties can be huge. It's natural to want to fit in and have a piece of Aunt Ethel's pecan pie like everyone else. We are all human. We all make mistakes and struggle with managing diabetes.

If things don't go according to your Hot Zone plan, don't feel guilty; just take action to redirect. If you ate a piece of cake, for example, increase your insulin to cover the excess carbohydrate or adjust carbohydrate intake at a later meal. Then give yourself a pat on the back for managing an unexpected situation.

Regardless of the type of diabetes you have, tomorrow you can start again. So get back on track and do your best. You can't change the past, but you can work toward a better future.

Keep Weight in Check

Try these tips to avoid the postseason diet frenzy:

Keep Track. Track food with a logbook or smartphone app. Stick to your blood glucose monitoring and diabetes care regimen no matter how stressful the holidays get.

To keep carbs and calories controlled, beware of the BLTs—bites, licks, and tastes of all those sweet treats out there. Those little bits add up and will affect your blood glucose level as well as how you feel.

Practice Moderation. Allow yourself one treat a day during the holidays, but count it toward your daily calories and carbohydrates. You may have to adjust your remaining caloric intake or exercise routine to burn it off.

Plate size can help you check portions. When you use small plates or small bowls, being more mindful about amounts is easy. In fact, using a 9-inch plate means you hardly have to think about it at all. But only fill it once!

The sheer abundance of food at parties can make it easy for carb consuming to get out of control. Don't finish food you don't like and do eat slowly. There's a temptation to pop a whole appetizer in your mouth because that's how they're constructed. It's better to take a few bites to extend the enjoyment.

Alcohol may seem like a stress reliever, but it can pack a lot of calories and lower blood glucose levels. Pace yourself with a glass of water or sparkling water between alcoholic drinks. Or skip the alcohol altogether.

Manage Food Police. Harassed by others who want to monitor your food choices? Just say, "Thank you for your concern. I have it under control."

Dealing with food pushers? Say, "I appreciate it, but I can't have that right now." Or ask for a to-go box.

If you're the host, challenge yourself to make healthy homemade foods rather than relying on fat-filled convenience items. If you're a guest, bring a healthy option to share.

TIME-SAVERS TO SWEAR BY

Less time prepping means more time for a peaceful walk or a relaxed coffee chat with a visiting relative. Here are a few time-savers to help you through the busy days.

Cooking
- Fill your pantry with healthful essentials so you aren't running to the store at the last minute. Stock up on low-sodium canned beans, tomatoes, and broth; herbs and spices; quick-cooking whole grains, nuts, and legumes; and condiments.
- Make appetizers, entrées, and desserts in advance and keep them in the freezer until needed.
- Devise a game plan and prep ingredients early.
- Double or triple recipes. Voilá—weekday meals!
- Utilize frozen vegetables and nutritious canned foods such as beans.

Baking
- Stock up on parchment paper and cooking spray.
- Instead of frosting, place a doily on baked goods and sprinkle with powdered sugar or cocoa powder.

- Whip up cookie, pie, and tart doughs ahead of time and keep in the freezer until you need them.

Shopping
- Research beforehand. Utilize the Internet to comparison shop—even better, see if any local grocery stores deliver.
- Find a good deal? Buy in bulk and give the same gift to a number of people.
- Get to the stores early. The later in the day you go, the busier stores will be. Go right when it opens and you'll practically have the place to yourself.
- Opt for free gift wrapping to save time. And be sure to label recipients so you don't forget.

TWEAKING TRADITIONS

It's not fair to have to give up your holiday favorites. Here are some healthy updates for treasured family food traditions.

 Replace sour cream dip served with potato chips with **Greek yogurt dip and cut veggies.**

 Replace mashed potatoes with **mashed cauliflower.**

 Replace canned cranberry sauce with **fresh cranberries mixed with chopped oranges**—zesty and super fresh!

 Replace eggnog with a glass of **warm apple cider.**

 Replace marshmallow-topped sweet potato casserole with cooked and **mashed butternut squash** served with orange slices.

EYE-OPENING
BREAKFASTS

1

Holiday breakfasts call for dishes a bit more special that you can sit down and enjoy with family and friends. These recipes highlight holiday flavors and feature traditional favorites in new and inventive ways, such as cranberry-topped pancakes, eggs Benedict made with quinoa cakes, and bacon and egg muffins.

Spiced Holiday Oatmeal

Spiced Holiday Oatmeal

35 g CARB

SERVES 10
HANDS ON 25 min.
TOTAL 1 hr.

- 1½ cups steel-cut oats
- 3 cups water
- 1 tsp. ground cinnamon
- ½ tsp. salt
- ½ tsp. ground allspice
- ½ tsp. ground ginger
- 1½ cups fat-free milk
- ½ cup packed brown sugar*
- 1 cup shredded carrots
- ½ cup snipped dried apricots
- 1 cup coarsely chopped, toasted pecans

1. Preheat oven to 350°F. Spread oats in a shallow baking pan. Bake about 10 minutes or until lightly toasted, stirring twice.
2. In a large saucepan combine toasted oats and the next five ingredients (through ginger). Bring just to boiling; reduce heat. Simmer, covered, 15 minutes. Stir in milk and brown sugar. Simmer, covered, 15 to 20 minutes more or just until oats are tender and liquid is nearly absorbed,
stirring occasionally. Stir in carrots and apricots.
3. Let stand, covered, 5 minutes. Spoon desired number of servings into cereal bowls. Sprinkle each with about 1½ Tbsp. of the pecans.

To Make Ahead Prepare as directed through Step 2. Let stand, covered, 20 minutes. If necessary, stir in additional milk, ¼ cup at a time, to reach desired consistency. Transfer to a bowl. Cover and chill up to 5 days. To reheat individual servings, spoon ½ cup oatmeal into a bowl; cover loosely with plastic wrap. Microwave on 50% power (medium) 1½ to 2 minutes or until heated, stirring once. Sprinkle with 1½ Tbsp. of the pecans.

PER SERVING *(½ cup each)* **CAL** 231, **FAT** 9 g (1 g sat. fat), **CHOL** 1 mg, **SODIUM** 146 mg, **CARB** 35 g (4 g fiber, 16 g sugars), **PRO** 6 g

*****Sugar Sub** Choose Splenda Brown Sugar Blend. Follow package directions to use ½ cup equivalent.

PER SERVING WITH SUB Same as above, except **CAL** 213, **CARB** 29 g (10 g sugars)

Poppy Seed Oat Waffles

26 g CARB

SERVES 8
HANDS ON 15 min.
TOTAL 30 min.

- ⅔ cup all-purpose flour
- ½ cup oat bran
- ⅓ cup whole wheat flour
- 2 Tbsp. flaxseed meal
- 1 Tbsp. sugar*
- 2 tsp. poppy seeds
- 1½ tsp. baking powder
- ¼ tsp. salt
- ¾ cup fat-free milk
- ¼ cup refrigerated or frozen egg product, thawed, or 1 egg, lightly beaten
- ¼ cup water
- 3 Tbsp. canola oil
- 1 tsp. vanilla
- 1 recipe Citrus Syrup

1. In a medium bowl stir together the first eight ingredients (through salt). Make a well in center of flour mixture.
2. In a small bowl combine the next five ingredients (through vanilla). Add to flour mixture; stir just until moistened (batter should be slightly lumpy).
3. Lightly grease and preheat a standard waffle baker. Pour half of the batter (about 1 cup) onto grid and spread to cover. Close lid; do not open until done. Bake until golden and crisp. Lift waffle off grid. Repeat with remaining batter. Serve with Citrus Syrup and remaining orange slices.

Citrus Syrup Peel and slice 2 oranges over a small saucepan, reserving juice. Add ½ cup water and 1 Tbsp. each cornstarch and honey. Cook and stir over medium until thick and bubbly. Add half of the orange slices (reserve remainder). Cook and stir 2 minutes more. Stir in 1 Tbsp. lemon juice.

PER SERVING *(1 waffle section + 2 Tbsp. syrup each)* **CAL** 173, **FAT** 7 g (1 g sat. fat), **CHOL** 0 mg, **SODIUM** 190 mg, **CARB** 26 g (3 g fiber, 8 g sugars), **PRO** 5 g

*****Sugar Sub** Choose Splenda Sugar Blend. Follow package directions to use 1 Tbsp. equivalent.

PER SERVING WITH SUB Same as above, except **CAL** 171, **SUGARS** 7 g

**Poppy Seed Oat Waffles
with Citrus Syrup**

Whole Wheat Gingerbread Pancakes

34 g CARB

SERVES 8
TOTAL 30 min.

- 1 recipe Spiced Cranberry Syrup
- ⅔ cup whole wheat flour
- ½ cup all-purpose flour
- 1 tsp. sugar*
- 1½ tsp. baking powder
- ½ tsp. baking soda
- 1 tsp. ground ginger
- ¼ tsp. salt
- ⅛ tsp. ground cloves
- 1 egg, lightly beaten
- ¾ cup buttermilk
- ¼ cup molasses
- 2 Tbsp. vegetable oil
  Nonstick cooking spray
- ½ cup frozen light whipped dessert topping, thawed (optional)

1. Prepare Spiced Cranberry Syrup. In a large bowl stir together the next eight ingredients (through cloves). In a medium bowl combine egg, buttermilk, molasses, and oil. Add egg mixture all at once to flour mixture. Stir just until moistened (batter should be slightly lumpy). Cover and chill up to 24 hours.

2. For each pancake, pour about 2 Tbsp. batter onto a hot, lightly greased griddle or heavy skillet; spread batter. (If batter is too thick, thin with a little additional buttermilk.) Cook over medium-low 2 to 3 minutes on each side or until pancakes are golden. Turn over when surfaces are bubbly and edges are slightly dry.

3. Serve with Spiced Cranberry Syrup. If desired, top with dessert topping.

Spiced Cranberry Syrup In a small saucepan combine 1 cup fresh or frozen cranberries, ⅓ cup pure maple syrup, 2 Tbsp. orange juice, and dash ground cinnamon. Cook and stir over medium-high until berries burst. Remove from heat. Mash berries slightly.

PER SERVING (2 pancakes + 1 Tbsp. syrup each) **CAL** 187, **FAT** 5 g (1 g sat. fat), **CHOL** 25 mg, **SODIUM** 281 mg, **CARB** 34 g (2 g fiber, 18 g sugars), **PRO** 4 g

*Sugar Sub Choose Splenda Sugar Blend. Follow package directions to use 1 tsp. equivalent.

PER SERVING WITH SUB Same as above, except **CAL** 186, **CARB** 33 g

Quinoa Cake Benedict with Roasted Tomatoes

27 g **CARB**

| **SERVES** 4 |
| **HANDS ON** 20 min. |
| **TOTAL** 50 min. |

- 3 egg whites, lightly beaten
- ½ cup soft whole wheat bread crumbs
- ¼ cup finely shredded Asiago cheese
- 2 Tbsp. chopped shallot
- ⅛ tsp. salt
- 1¾ cups cooked quinoa
- 4 tsp. olive oil
- 2 cups grape tomatoes
- 1 medium shallot, thinly sliced
- ¼ tsp. salt
- ¼ tsp. black pepper
- 2 cups baby arugula or baby kale
- 2 tsp. champagne vinegar or white wine vinegar
- 1 recipe Poached Eggs

1. Preheat oven to 400°F. In a bowl combine the first five ingredients (through ⅛ tsp. salt). Stir in quinoa. Let stand 20 minutes. Form mixture into four 3½-inch-diameter patties. In a 10-inch nonstick skillet heat 2 tsp. of the oil over medium. Carefully add patties. Cook patties about 5 minutes per side or until golden, turning carefully once.

2. Meanwhile, in a foil-lined shallow baking pan combine the tomatoes and shallot. Drizzle with the remaining 2 tsp. olive oil; stir to coat. Sprinkle with salt and pepper. Roast 12 to 15 minutes or until skins start to burst, gently stirring once. Remove from oven. Cool 5 minutes. Add arugula and sprinkle with vinegar; toss to combine.

3. To serve, arrange quinoa cakes on plates. Top with Poached Eggs and tomato mixture.

Poached Eggs In a 10-inch skillet combine 4 cups water and 1 Tbsp. vinegar. Bring to boiling; reduce heat to simmering (bubbles should begin to break the surface of the water). Break an egg into a cup and slip egg into the simmering water. Repeat with three more eggs, allowing each egg an equal amount of space in the skillet. Simmer eggs, uncovered, 3 to 5 minutes or until the whites are completely set and yolks begin to thicken but are not hard. Using a slotted spoon, remove eggs from skillet. Season with salt and black pepper.

Tip For cooked quinoa, in a medium saucepan combine 1 cup water and ½ cup uncooked quinoa, rinsed and drained. Bring to boiling; reduce heat. Cover and simmer about 15 minutes or until quinoa is tender. Drain if necessary. Cool.

PER SERVING *(1 cake + 1 egg + ⅔ cup tomato mixture each)* **CAL** 302, **FAT** 14 g (4 g sat. fat), **CHOL** 193 mg, **SODIUM** 520 mg, **CARB** 27 g (4 g fiber, 5 g sugars), **PRO** 16 g

Quinoa Cake Benedict with Roasted Tomatoes

Bacon-and-Egg Muffins

17g
CARB

SERVES 12
HANDS ON 30 min.
TOTAL 50 min.

- 4 slices lower-sodium, less-fat bacon, cut into thirds
- 5 eggs
- 2 Tbsp. water
  Dash black pepper
  Nonstick cooking spray
- 1 cup all-purpose flour

- ½ cup yellow cornmeal
- 2 Tbsp. sugar*
- 2 tsp. baking powder
- ¼ tsp. salt
- 1 cup low-fat milk (1%)
- 3 Tbsp. vegetable oil or melted butter
- 3 Tbsp. unsweetened applesauce
- ½ cup shredded reduced-fat cheddar cheese (2 oz.)
  Pure maple syrup (optional)

1. Preheat oven to 400°F. In a 10-inch skillet cook bacon just until it begins to crisp. Drain, reserving drippings. Return 2 tsp. of the drippings to the skillet. For scrambled eggs, in a small bowl beat three of the eggs, the water, and pepper. Cook egg mixture in hot skillet over medium, without stirring, until mixture begins to set on bottom and around edges. With a large spatula, lift and fold the partially cooked egg mixture so the uncooked

portion flows underneath. Continue cooking over medium until egg mixture is cooked through but is still glossy and moist. Transfer to a bowl.
2. Coat twelve 2½-inch muffin cups with cooking spray. In a medium bowl stir together the next five ingredients (through salt). Make a well in the center of the flour mixture. In a separate bowl whisk together the remaining two eggs, the milk, oil, and applesauce. Add egg mixture all at once to flour mixture. Stir just until moistened (batter should be lumpy). Fold in scrambled eggs and cheese. Spoon batter into muffin cups (cups will be full). Place one bacon piece on each muffin.
3. Bake 15 to 17 minutes or until light brown and a toothpick inserted in centers comes out clean. Cool in cups on a wire rack 5 minutes. Run a small metal spatula or table knife around edges of muffins to loosen; remove from cups. If desired, serve warm with maple syrup.

PER SERVING *(1 muffin each)* **CAL** 159, **FAT** 7 g (2 g sat. fat), **CHOL** 83 mg, **SODIUM** 231 mg, **CARB** 17 g (1 g fiber, 4 g sugars), **PRO** 7 g

*Sugar Sub Choose Splenda Sugar Blend. Follow package directions to use 2 Tbsp. equivalent.

PER SERVING WITH SUB Same as above, except **CAL** 156, **CARB** 16 g (3 g sugars)

Sweet Potato Egg Bake

QUICK TIP ⌃
Save prep time by using packaged sliced mushrooms and baby spinach so you can skip slicing and tearing steps.

Sweet Potato Egg Bake

12 g
CARB

SERVES 9	
HANDS ON 20 min.	
TOTAL 1 hr. 20 min.	

Nonstick cooking spray
6 slices lower-sodium, less-fat bacon
2 cups sliced fresh cremini or button mushrooms
1 cup sliced leek (white part only)
1 Tbsp. olive oil
2 cups torn fresh spinach
1 large (9 oz.) sweet potato, peeled and coarsely shredded (3 cups)
2 Tbsp. all-purpose flour
¾ cup shredded reduced-fat Swiss cheese or 3 slices reduced-fat Swiss cheese, thinly sliced into shreds
4 eggs
4 egg whites
1¼ cups fat-free milk
¼ salt
¼ black pepper

1. Preheat oven to 350°F. Coat a 2-qt. square baking dish with cooking spray. In a 12-inch nonstick skillet cook bacon over medium until crisp. Transfer to paper towels to drain. Crumble bacon.
2. Wipe out skillet. In the same skillet cook mushrooms and leek in hot oil over medium about 6 minutes or until tender, stirring occasionally. Stir in spinach. Cook 2 minutes more or until wilted.
3. In a bowl toss together sweet potato and flour to coat. Arrange in prepared baking dish. Sprinkle with bacon, cooked vegetables, and cheese.
4. In a bowl whisk together the remaining ingredients. Pour over layers in dish. Bake, uncovered, 45 to 50 minutes or until a knife inserted near the center comes out clean.

PER SERVING (¾ cup each) **CAL** 153, **FAT** 7 g (3 g sat. fat), **CHOL** 92 mg, **SODIUM** 221 mg, **CARB** 12 g (1 g fiber, 4 g sugars), **PRO** 12 g

Fennel and Asparagus Pie

Fennel and Asparagus Pie

28 g
CARB

SERVES 6	
HANDS ON 30 min.	
TOTAL 50 min.	

½ of a 14.1-oz. pkg. (1 crust) rolled refrigerated unbaked piecrust
1 medium fennel bulb
1 lb. asparagus spears, trimmed and cut into 1-inch pieces
½ cup chopped onion
¾ cup fat-free milk
2 Tbsp. all-purpose flour
3 eggs
1 Tbsp. snipped fresh basil or 1 tsp. dried basil, crushed
½ tsp. salt
⅛ tsp. black pepper
1 cup shredded part-skim mozzarella cheese (4 oz.)

1. Preheat oven to 425°F. Let piecrust stand according to package directions. On a lightly floured surface roll piecrust into a 13-inch circle. Transfer to a 9-inch pie plate; trim to ½ inch beyond edge. Fold under extra pastry and crimp edge. Do not prick pastry. Line pastry with a double thickness of foil. Bake 8 minutes; remove foil. Bake 4 to 5 minutes more or until set and dry. Remove from oven. Reduce oven temperature to 375°F.
2. Meanwhile, trim fennel, reserving some of the fronds. Thinly slice fennel. In a covered medium saucepan cook sliced fennel, asparagus, and onion in a small amount of boiling water 4 to 6 minutes or just until tender; drain.
3. In a bowl whisk together milk and flour until smooth. Whisk in the next four ingredients (through pepper) until combined. Spoon fennel mixture into partially baked piecrust; sprinkle with cheese. Gradually pour in egg mixture.
4. Bake 30 to 35 minutes or until egg mixture is set in center. If necessary to prevent overbrowning, cover edge of pie loosely with foil the last 5 to 10 minutes of baking. Let stand 10 minutes before serving. Top with reserved fennel fronds and, if desired, additional fresh basil.

PER SERVING (1 wedge each) **CAL** 290, **FAT** 15 g (6 g sat. fat), **CHOL** 122 mg, **SODIUM** 524 mg, **CARB** 28 g (3 g fiber, 4 g sugars), **PRO** 12 g

Bacon, Potato, and Kale Frittata

Crustless Spinach and Mushroom Quiche

11 g
CARB

SERVES 8
HANDS ON 20 min.
SLOW COOK 5 hr.

Disposable slow cooker liner
- 1 10-oz. pkg. frozen chopped spinach, thawed and well drained
- 4 slices turkey bacon
- 1 Tbsp. olive oil
- 2 cups coarsely chopped portobello mushrooms
- ½ cup chopped red sweet pepper
- 1 cup shredded Gruyère or Swiss cheese (4 oz.)
- 8 eggs
- 2 cups reduced-fat milk
- 1 Tbsp. snipped fresh chives or 1 tsp. dried chives
- ¼ tsp. salt
- ¼ tsp. black pepper
- ½ cup reduced-fat biscuit mix

1. Line a 3½- or 4-qt. slow cooker with disposable liner. Lightly coat liner with *nonstick cooking spray*. Press spinach with clean paper towels to remove as much liquid as possible.
2. In an 8-inch skillet cook bacon until crisp; drain and crumble bacon. Discard drippings. In the same skillet heat oil over medium. Add mushrooms and sweet pepper; cook and stir until tender. Remove from heat. Stir in spinach and cheese.
3. In a bowl lightly beat eggs with a fork. Stir in milk, chives, salt, and black pepper. Stir into spinach mixture in skillet. Gently fold in biscuit mix. Pour mixture into prepared slow cooker. Sprinkle with bacon.
4. Cover and cook on low 5 to 6 hours or high 2 to 3 hours or until a knife inserted into center comes out clean. Turn off slow cooker. If possible, remove crockery liner from cooker. Cool 15 to 30 minutes.
5. To serve, lift disposable liner from cooker onto a cutting board. Remove quiche from liner and cut into wedges.

PER SERVING *(1 wedge each)* **CAL** 243, **FAT** 15 g (6 g sat. fat), **CHOL** 237 mg, **SODIUM** 455 mg, **CARB** 11 g (1 g fiber, 5 g sugars), **PRO** 17 g

Bacon, Potato, and Kale Frittata

13 g
CARB

SERVES 6
TOTAL 30 min.

- 12 oz. tiny red-skin new potatoes, quartered
- 6 slices lower-sodium, less-fat bacon, coarsely chopped
- 2 cups chopped fresh kale
- ½ cup coarsely chopped onion
- 8 eggs, lightly beaten
- ¼ tsp. salt
- ¼ tsp. black pepper

1. In a covered medium saucepan cook potatoes in enough boiling lightly salted water to cover about 10 minutes or just until tender. Drain.
2. Meanwhile, preheat broiler. In a 10-inch broilerproof skillet with flared sides cook bacon over medium-high until starting to crisp. Add kale and onion; cook about 5 minutes or until onion is tender. Stir in the cooked potatoes.

3. In a bowl whisk together eggs, salt, and pepper. Pour egg mixture over potato mixture. Cook over medium-low. As mixture sets, run a spatula around edge of skillet, lifting egg mixture so uncooked portion flows underneath. Continue cooking and lifting edges until egg mixture is almost set (surface will be moist).
4. Place skillet under broiler 4 to 5 inches from heat. Broil 1 to 2 minutes or until top is set and no longer wet. (Or preheat oven to 400°F and bake about 5 minutes or until top is set and no longer wet.) Let stand 5 minutes. Slide frittata out of pan onto a serving platter. Cut into six wedges.

PER SERVING *(1 wedge each)* **CAL** 175, **FAT** 8 g (3 g sat. fat), **CHOL** 251 mg, **SODIUM** 281 mg, **CARB** 13 g (2 g fiber, 2 g sugars), **PRO** 13 g

QUICK TIP Cut the fat by using 2 cups refrigerated or frozen egg product, thawed, for the whole eggs.

**Crustless Spinach
and Mushroom Quiche**

Savory Breakfast Bread Pudding

11g CARB

SERVES 6
HANDS ON 30 min.
TOTAL 1 hr. 10 min.

- 5 cups ½-inch cubes seeded artisan-style multigrain bread
  Nonstick cooking spray
- 3 tsp. canola oil
- 1 cup chopped cremini mushrooms
- ½ cup finely chopped red sweet pepper
- ½ cup thinly sliced leek
- 3 egg yolks
- 1 cup fat-free milk
- ⅓ cup reduced-sodium chicken or vegetable broth
- 1 tsp. snipped fresh dill weed or ½ tsp. dried dill weed
- ¼ tsp. black pepper
- 4 oz. Gruyère or Swiss cheese, finely shredded (¾ cup)
- 4 egg whites
- ½ cup sliced shallots
- ¾ cup halved grape tomatoes
- ¾ cup bite-size strips red sweet peppers

1. Preheat oven to 300°F. In a 15×10-inch baking pan spread bread cubes in a single layer. Bake 10 to 15 minutes or until dry, stirring once or twice. Remove pan from oven. Increase oven temperature to 375°F. Lightly coat six 8-oz. ramekins or custard cups with cooking spray.

2. In a 10-inch nonstick skillet heat 2 tsp. of the oil over medium. Add mushrooms, the ½ cup sweet pepper, and leek; cook and stir about 4 minutes or until tender.

3. In a large bowl lightly beat egg yolks. Whisk in milk, broth, dill, and black pepper. Add bread cubes, mushroom mixture, and cheese; toss to combine. In a second bowl beat egg whites with a mixer on high until soft peaks form (tips curl). Gently fold egg whites into bread mixture. Spoon bread mixture into prepared ramekins. Arrange ramekins in baking pan used to dry bread cubes.

4. Bake about 20 minutes or until puffed, golden, and a knife inserted in center comes out clean.

5. Meanwhile, wipe out skillet. Add the shallots and remaining 1 tsp. oil. Cook over medium-high about 3 minutes or until golden, stirring occasionally. Add tomatoes and ¾ cup peppers; cook about 4 minutes or until softened, gently stirring occasionally.

6. Spoon tomato mixture over puddings and top with additional fresh dill weed.

PER SERVING *(1 individual bread pudding + ¼ cup topper each)* **CAL** 192, **FAT** 11 g (5 g sat. fat), **CHOL** 114 mg, **SODIUM** 244 mg, **CARB** 11 g (2 g fiber, 6 g sugars), **PRO** 13 g

Savory Breakfast Bread Pudding

Egg and Squash Boats

17g CARB

SERVES 4
TOTAL 25 min.

- 2 8-oz. delicata squash
- 5 Tbsp. water
- 1 cup frozen loose-pack brown rice
- 4 links refrigerated fully cooked chicken breakfast sausage, chopped
- ¼ cup finely shredded Parmesan cheese
- ½ tsp. dried sage, crushed
- ⅛ tsp. black pepper
  Nonstick cooking spray
- 4 eggs
- 1 Tbsp. balsamic glaze

Egg and Squash Boats

1. Cut squash in half lengthwise; remove and discard seeds and strings. In a 2-qt. square baking dish arrange two squash halves, cut sides down; add 2 Tbsp. of the water. Cover with vented plastic wrap. Microwave 4 to 6 minutes or until squash is just tender; keep warm. Repeat with the remaining squash halves.

2. In a bowl stir together the next five ingredients (through pepper). Cover and microwave about 1½ minutes or until heated.

3. Meanwhile, coat a 10-inch nonstick skillet with cooking spray; heat skillet over medium-low. Break eggs into skillet. Cook 3 to 4 minutes or until whites are firm. Add the remaining 1 Tbsp. water to skillet; cover and cook 4 to 5 minutes or until yolks begin to thicken but are not hard.

4. To serve, fill squash halves with rice mixture. Arrange a cooked egg on each. Drizzle with balsamic glaze and, if desired, sprinkle with additional pepper.

PER SERVING *(1 boat each)* **CAL** 216, **FAT** 9 g (4 g sat. fat), **CHOL** 215 mg, **SODIUM** 327 mg, **CARB** 17 g (2 g fiber, 8 g sugars), **PRO** 17 g

Smoked Salmon and Red Pepper Frittata

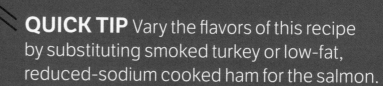

QUICK TIP Vary the flavors of this recipe by substituting smoked turkey or low-fat, reduced-sodium cooked ham for the salmon.

Smoked Salmon and Red Pepper Frittata

5g CARB | **SERVES** 6
HANDS ON 15 min.
TOTAL 30 min.

- 8 eggs, lightly beaten
- ¾ cup low-fat cottage cheese or crumbled reduced-fat feta cheese
- 1 tsp. herbes de Provence or Italian seasoning, crushed, or ½ tsp. dried dill weed
- ¼ tsp. black pepper
  Nonstick cooking spray
- ½ cup chopped red onion
- 2 cloves garlic, minced
- 4 cups baby spinach or torn spinach
- ½ cup thinly sliced seeded mini red sweet peppers
- 1 oz. thinly sliced smoked salmon (lox-style); smoked turkey; or low-fat, reduced-sodium cooked boneless ham, chopped

1. Preheat broiler. In a bowl combine eggs, cottage cheese, herbes de Provence, and black pepper.
2. Coat an unheated 10-inch cast-iron or broilerproof nonstick skillet with cooking spray. Preheat skillet over medium. Add onion and garlic. Cook about 4 minutes or until onion is just tender, stirring occasionally. Stir in spinach; cook about 1 minute more or until wilted.
3. Pour egg mixture over vegetables in skillet. Cook over medium. As mixture sets, run a spatula around edge of skillet, lifting egg mixture so uncooked portion flows underneath. Continue cooking and lifting edges until mixture is almost set. Sprinkle sliced red sweet peppers and salmon on top.
4. Place skillet under broiler 4 to 5 inches from heat. Broil about 2 minutes or until just set. Let stand 1 minute. Cut into wedges.

PER SERVING *(1 wedge each)* **CAL** 141, **FAT** 7 g (2 g sat. fat), **CHOL** 284 mg, **SODIUM** 333 mg, **CARB** 5 g (1 g fiber, 2 g sugars), **PRO** 14 g

Breakfast Ham and Egg Cups

Breakfast Ham and Egg Cups

2g CARB | **SERVES** 8
HANDS ON 20 min.
TOTAL 40 min.

  Nonstick cooking spray
- 8 thin slices deli-style cooked ham
- ¼ cup shredded Italian cheese blend or mozzarella cheese (1 oz.)
- 8 eggs
  Black pepper
- 8 tsp. basil pesto (optional)
- 8 cherry or grape tomatoes, halved

1. Preheat oven to 350°F. Coat eight 2½-inch muffin cups with cooking spray. Gently press ham slices onto bottoms and up sides of prepared muffin cups, ruffling edges. Sprinkle with cheese.
2. Break eggs, one at a time, into a measuring cup; slip each into a muffin cup. Sprinkle with pepper. Top with pesto (if using) and tomatoes.
3. Bake 18 to 20 minutes or until whites are completely set and yolks are thickened. Cool in muffin cups on a wire rack 3 minutes. Remove from muffin cups; serve warm.

PER SERVING *(1 egg cup each)* **CAL** 145, **FAT** 10 g (3 g sat. fat), **CHOL** 202 mg, **SODIUM** 413 mg, **CARB** 2 g (1 g fiber, 1 g sugars), **PRO** 11 g

Nutty Chocolate Granola Bars

Nutty Chocolate Granola Bars

24 g
CARB

SERVES 12
HANDS ON 15 min.
TOTAL 35 min.

- 1 cup regular rolled oats
- ¼ cup slivered almonds, chopped
- ½ cup natural creamy peanut butter
- ⅓ cup honey
- ¼ cup refrigerated or frozen egg product, thawed, or 1 egg, lightly beaten
- 1 Tbsp. canola oil
- ½ cup oat bran
- ¼ cup almond meal
- ¼ cup chia seed powder or flaxseed meal
- ¼ tsp. salt
- ⅓ cup miniature semisweet chocolate pieces

1. Preheat oven to 325°F. In a shallow baking pan combine oats and almonds. Bake about 10 minutes or until lightly toasted, stirring twice; cool.
2. Meanwhile, in a large bowl combine the next four ingredients (through oil). Stir in oat mixture and the next four ingredients (through salt) until combined. Stir in chocolate pieces.
3. Line a baking sheet with parchment paper. On the prepared baking sheet shape oat mixture into a 6-inch square; cut square in half. Cut each half crosswise into 1-inch strips (12 bars total). Separate bars, leaving about 1 inch between bars.
4. Bake 10 to 12 minutes or until bars are set and edges are light brown. Remove; cool on a wire rack. If desired, wrap individual bars with plastic wrap.

To Store Place wrapped bars in an airtight container at room temperature up to 2 days or freeze up to 3 months.

PER SERVING *(1 bar each)* **CAL** 221, **FAT** 13 g (3 g sat. fat), **CHOL** 0 mg, **SODIUM** 105 mg, **CARB** 24 g (4 g fiber, 13 g sugars), **PRO** 7 g

Lemon Honey Parfaits with Blueberries

Lemon Honey Parfaits with Blueberries

31 g
CARB

SERVES 4
HANDS ON 20 min.
TOTAL 50 min.

- 1 lemon
- 1 envelope unflavored gelatin
- ¼ tsp. kosher salt
- ½ cup boiling water
- 5 Tbsp. honey
- 1 cup plain low-fat yogurt
- 1 cup fresh blueberries

1. Remove 1½ tsp. zest and squeeze 1 tsp. juice from lemon. In a small bowl stir gelatin and salt into the boiling water until dissolved. Stir in lemon zest and ¼ cup of the honey. Stir in yogurt.
2. Spoon yogurt mixture into stemmed glasses. Chill at least 30 minutes or until set.
3. In a bowl combine lemon juice and the remaining 1 Tbsp. honey. Stir in blueberries. Top parfaits with blueberry mixture and, if desired, additional lemon zest.

PER SERVING *(1 parfait each)* **CAL** 145, **FAT** 1 g (1 g sat. fat), **CHOL** 4 mg, **SODIUM** 115 mg, **CARB** 31 g (1 g fiber, 30 g sugars), **PRO** 6 g

2

TASTY

PARTY BITES

Get out of the holiday party rut with creative and fresh appetizer recipes that won't bust your dietary budget. Each is properly portioned; light in calories, fat, and carbs; and super tasty. Let guests crunch, dip, or sip their way through this selection of cold and hot tidbits all season.

Pomegranate,
Cranberry, and
Brie Bruschetta

Pomegranate, Cranberry, and Brie Bruschetta

8 g CARB

SERVES 16
HANDS ON 30 min.
TOTAL 42 min.

- ¾ cup pomegranate seeds
- ½ cup chopped fresh or frozen cranberries, thawed
- 2 Tbsp. sugar*
- 1 tsp. orange zest
  Dash salt
- 6 oz. baguette-style French bread, cut diagonally into 16 slices
  Nonstick cooking spray
- ⅛ tsp. black pepper
- 1 6-oz. log Brie cheese, cut diagonally into 16 slices
- 1 Tbsp. finely snipped fresh basil

1. In a small bowl combine the first five ingredients (through salt). Cover and chill up to 3 days.
2. To serve, preheat oven to 350°F. Line a 15×10-inch baking pan with parchment paper. Place bread slices in pan. Lightly coat both sides of bread with cooking spray; sprinkle with pepper. Bake 8 minutes, turning once. Top with cheese. Bake about 4 minutes more or until cheese is softened.
3. Stir basil into pomegranate mixture and spoon on top of bread slices. Serve warm.

PER SERVING *(1 bruschetta each)* **CAL** 77, **FAT** 3 g (2 g sat. fat), **CHOL** 8 mg, **SODIUM** 114 mg, **CARB** 8 g (0 g fiber, 2 g sugars), **PRO** 2 g

*Sugar Sub Choose Splenda Sugar Blend. Follow package directions to use 2 Tbsp. equivalent.

PER SERVING WITH SUB Same as above, except **CAL** 75

Cherry-Chicken Salad Bites

Cherry-Chicken Salad Bites

5 g CARB

SERVES 16
HANDS ON 30 min.
TOTAL 40 min.

- ½ cup water
- 6 Tbsp. light butter with canola oil
- ⅛ tsp. salt
- ½ cup all-purpose flour
- ¼ cup white whole wheat flour
- 2 eggs, lightly beaten
- 3 Tbsp. finely chopped fennel (reserve fronds)
- ½ cup finely chopped cooked chicken breast
- 3 Tbsp. snipped dried cherries and/or dried apricots
- 2 Tbsp. plain fat-free Greek yogurt
- 2 Tbsp. chopped toasted pecans
- 1 Tbsp. buttermilk
  Dash salt
  Dash black pepper

1. Preheat oven to 425°F. Line a large baking sheet with parchment paper. In a small saucepan combine the first three ingredients (through ⅛ tsp. salt). Bring to boiling. Add both flours all at once; stir vigorously. Cook and stir until mixture forms a ball that doesn't separate. Remove from heat; let cool 5 minutes.
2. Transfer mixture to a large bowl. Add eggs, one at a time, beating with a mixer after each addition until smooth. Pipe dough in 16 mounds 2 inches apart onto prepared baking sheet.
3. Bake 10 minutes. Reduce oven temperature to 350°F. Bake 18 to 20 minutes more or until golden and firm. Poke each puff with a toothpick to allow steam to escape. Cool completely.
4. For filling, snip 2 tsp. of the fennel fronds. In a medium bowl combine snipped fennel fronds, chopped fennel, and the remaining ingredients. Cover and chill up to 3 days.
5. To serve, cut tops from puffs. Spoon about 1 Tbsp. filling onto the bottom of each puff. Replace tops.

To Make Ahead Prepare puffs as directed through Step 3. Place cooled puffs in an airtight container and freeze up to 1 month.

PER SERVING *(1 puff each)* **CAL** 66, **FAT** 3 g (1 g sat. fat), **CHOL** 29 mg, **SODIUM** 94 mg, **CARB** 5 g (0 g fiber, 1 g sugars), **PRO** 3 g

Baked Coconut Shrimp with Sweet Chili Dipping Sauce

10 g CARB

SERVES 6
HANDS ON 20 min.
TOTAL 30 min.

- 12 medium fresh or frozen shrimp in shells (about 5 oz.)
  Nonstick cooking spray
- 3 Tbsp. all-purpose flour
- ¼ tsp. sea salt
- 2 egg whites, lightly beaten
- ½ cup unsweetened shredded coconut
- ¼ cup panko bread crumbs
- ¼ cup Asian sweet chili sauce

1. Thaw shrimp, if frozen. Peel and devein shrimp, leaving tails intact if desired. Rinse shrimp; pat dry.

2. Preheat oven to 450°F. Line a baking sheet with foil; coat foil with cooking spray. In a shallow dish stir together flour and salt. Place egg whites in a second shallow dish. In a third shallow dish combine coconut and bread crumbs.

3. Dip shrimp in flour mixture, then in egg whites to coat. Dip in coconut mixture, turning and pressing to coat. Place on prepared baking sheet. Coat shrimp with cooking spray.

4. Bake 7 to 10 minutes or until shrimp are opaque and coating is golden. If desired, thread shrimp onto small wooden skewers. Serve with chili sauce.

PER SERVING (2 shrimp + 2 tsp. sauce each)
CAL 106, **FAT** 4 g (4 g sat. fat), **CHOL** 34 mg, **SODIUM** 244 mg, **CARB** 10 g (0 g fiber, 4 g sugars), **PRO** 6 g

Thai Peanut Chicken Wonton Cups

6 g
CARB

SERVES 24
HANDS ON 20 min.
TOTAL 35 min.

Nonstick cooking spray
24 wonton wrappers
⅓ cup peanut satay sauce
3 Tbsp. refrigerated unsweetened coconut milk beverage
2 cups shredded cabbage with carrot (coleslaw mix)
1 cup chopped cooked chicken breast
⅓ cup snipped fresh cilantro
2 Tbsp. unsalted peanuts, chopped
1 Tbsp. crushed red pepper (optional)
Sriracha sauce (optional)

1. Preheat oven to 375°F. Lightly coat twenty-four 1¾-inch muffin cups with cooking spray. Press wonton wrappers onto bottoms and up sides of prepared muffin cups. Coat wonton cups with cooking spray. Bake 7 to 8 minutes or until edges are brown. Cool in pan on a wire rack.
2. In a medium bowl combine the peanut sauce and coconut milk. Add the coleslaw mix and chicken; toss to coat.
3. Fill wonton cups with chicken mixture. Top with cilantro, peanuts, and, if desired, crushed red pepper and sriracha sauce. Serve immediately.

To Make Ahead The chicken mixture can be made ahead and stored in a covered container in the refrigerator up to 2 days. The wonton cups are best served the same day they are baked. Assemble wonton cups just before serving.

PER SERVING (1 wonton cup each) CAL 50, FAT 1 g (0 g sat. fat), CHOL 6 mg, SODIUM 77 mg, CARB 6 g (0 g fiber, 1 g sugars), PRO 3 g

Almond-Thyme Party Toasts with Goat Cheese

8 g
CARB

SERVES 16
TOTAL 15 min.

16 slices party pumpernickel or rye bread, toasted
4 oz. soft goat cheese (chèvre)
¼ cup pomegranate seeds
¼ cup finely chopped almonds
2 Tbsp. fresh thyme leaves
2 Tbsp. honey

1. Spread bread slices with cheese. Sprinkle with pomegranate seeds, almonds, and thyme. Before serving, drizzle with honey.

PER SERVING (1 toast each) CAL 66, FAT 3 g (1 g sat. fat), CHOL 3 mg, SODIUM 97 mg, CARB 8 g (1 g fiber, 3 g sugars), PRO 3 g

QUICK TIP Use a long toothpick or decorative party pick to skewer each fajita slice. The picks hold them together and make it easier to dip the bites in salsa.

Zesty Fajita Bites

Zesty Fajita Bites

5g CARB

SERVES 30
HANDS ON 25 min.
SLOW COOK 7 hr.

Nonstick cooking spray
- 1½ lb. bone-in chicken thighs, skin removed
- ½ cup spicy brown mustard
- ½ cup water
- 2 tsp. fajita seasoning or salt-free fiesta lime seasoning blend
- 6 7- to 8-inch flour tortillas, warmed
- 1 cup red, green, and/or yellow sweet pepper strips
  Sliced green onions (optional)
  Snipped fresh cilantro and/or salsa (optional)

1. Lightly coat a 10-inch skillet with cooking spray; heat skillet over medium-high. Add chicken and cook until browned on both sides. Drain off fat. Transfer chicken to a 1½-qt. slow cooker.
2. In a bowl combine mustard, the water, and fajita seasoning. Pour mixture over chicken, stirring to coat.
3. Cover and cook on low 7 to 8 hours or high 3½ to 4 hours. Remove chicken from cooker. Discard cooking juices. Shred chicken using two forks; discard bones.
4. To serve, divide shredded chicken among tortillas. Top with sweet pepper strips and, if desired, green onions. Roll up tortillas. Using a serrated knife, cut each roll-up into five slices. If desired, serve with cilantro and/or salsa.

Tip If using salt-free fiesta lime seasoning blend, add ½ tsp. salt.

To Warm Tortillas Preheat oven to 350°F. Stack tortillas and wrap tightly in foil. Bake about 10 minutes or until heated.

PER SERVING (1 fajita bite each) **CAL** 44, **FAT** 1 g (0 g sat. fat), **CHOL** 13 mg, **SODIUM** 129 mg, **CARB** 5 g (1 g fiber, 0 g sugars), **PRO** 3 g

Parmesan-Crusted Chicken Nuggets

Parmesan-Crusted Chicken Nuggets

2g CARB

SERVES 40
HANDS ON 20 min.
TOTAL 30 min.

- 1¼ lb. skinless, boneless chicken breast halves
- 2 egg whites
- 1 cup finely shredded Parmigiano-Reggiano cheese or Parmesan cheese (4 oz.)
- 1 cup panko bread crumbs
- ¼ tsp. black pepper
  Nonstick cooking spray
- 1 cup marinara sauce, warmed

1. Preheat oven to 425°F. Line a large baking sheet with parchment paper. Cut chicken into 1-inch pieces.
2. In a bowl whisk egg whites until frothy. In another bowl combine cheese, bread crumbs, and pepper.
3. Add chicken to egg whites; toss to coat. Transfer chicken, a few pieces at a time, to cheese mixture; toss gently to coat (if necessary, press lightly to adhere). Place chicken on the prepared baking sheet. Lightly coat chicken with cooking spray.
4. Bake 10 to 15 minutes or until chicken is no longer pink and coating is lightly browned. Serve marinara sauce with chicken for dipping.

PER SERVING (1 nugget each) **CAL** 34, **FAT** 1 g (0 g sat. fat), **CHOL** 10 mg, **SODIUM** 77 mg, **CARB** 2 g (0 g fiber, 0 g sugars), **PRO** 5 g

Marinated Shrimp Scampi

1g
CARB

SERVES	10
HANDS ON	35 min.
TOTAL	1 hr. 35 min.

- 2 lb. fresh or frozen extra-jumbo shrimp in shells (32 to 40)
- ¼ cup olive oil
- ¼ cup dry white wine
- 6 cloves garlic, minced
- 2 tsp. lemon zest
- ½ tsp. sea salt
- ½ tsp. crushed red pepper
- 2 Tbsp. snipped fresh Italian parsley
  Lemon wedges

1. Thaw shrimp, if frozen. Peel and devein shrimp, leaving tails intact if desired. Rinse shrimp; pat dry. Place shrimp in a resealable plastic bag set in a shallow dish.

2. For marinade, in a small bowl combine next six ingredients (through crushed red pepper). Pour marinade over shrimp. Seal bag; turn to coat shrimp. Marinate in the refrigerator 1 hour, turning bag once.

3. Preheat broiler. Drain shrimp, reserving marinade. Place shrimp on unheated rack of a broiler pan. Broil 4 to 5 inches from heat 4 to 6 minutes or until shrimp are opaque, turning and brushing once with marinade. Discard any remaining marinade.

4. To serve, mound shrimp onto a platter. Sprinkle with parsley and serve with lemon wedges. If desired, use cocktail picks for serving.

PER SERVING (3 or 4 shrimp each) **CAL** 124, **FAT** 6 g (1 g sat. fat), **CHOL** 127 mg, **SODIUM** 207 mg, **CARB** 1 g (0 g fiber, 0 g sugars), **PRO** 16 g

Salmon Rillettes

6g
CARB

SERVES	12
HANDS ON	20 min.
SLOW COOK	1 hr. 45 min.

- 1 lb. fresh skinless salmon fillets
- ½ tsp. salt
- ¼ tsp. black pepper
- 3 large leeks, trimmed and halved lengthwise
- ½ cup water
- 1 8-oz. tub light cream cheese spread with garden vegetables
- ¼ cup snipped fresh chives
- 2 heads Belgian endive, separated into leaves (about 24)
  Lemon wedges (optional)

1. Rinse salmon; pat dry with paper towels. Sprinkle salmon with salt and pepper. In a 4-qt. slow cooker combine leeks and the water. Place salmon on top of leeks, cutting to fit if necessary.

2. Cover and cook on low 1¾ to 2 hours or until salmon flakes easily. Remove salmon from cooker; discard leeks and cooking liquid. Cool salmon slightly. Coarsely flake salmon using a fork.

3. In a medium bowl combine cream cheese spread and 3 Tbsp. of the chives. Stir in salmon. Cover and chill 2 to 8 hours.

4. To serve, mound salmon mixture onto endive leaves. Sprinkle with the remaining 1 Tbsp. chives. If desired, serve with lemon wedges.

PER SERVING (2 rillettes each) **CAL** 111, **FAT** 5 g (2 g sat. fat), **CHOL** 32 mg, **SODIUM** 236 mg, **CARB** 6 g (1 g fiber, 2 g sugars), **PRO** 9 g

Marinated Shrimp Scampi

Salmon Rillettes

QUICK TIP Choose thick asparagus spears so they are crisp-tender and hold up to dipping after roasting.

Panko Roasted Asparagus

Roasted Pepper Soup Shooters

17 g CARB

SERVES 6
HANDS ON 25 min.
TOTAL 1 hr.

- 3 yellow sweet peppers
- ½ cup chopped onion
- 2 cloves garlic, minced
- 1 tsp. olive oil
- 2½ to 3 cups reduced-sodium vegetable broth
- 1 cup chopped, peeled sweet potato
- 2 Tbsp. snipped fresh basil
- 2 Tbsp. white balsamic vinegar or white wine vinegar
  Grape tomatoes, halved
  Small fresh basil leaves

1. Preheat oven to 425°F. Quarter sweet peppers lengthwise; remove and discard stems, seeds, and membranes. Place pepper quarters, cut sides down, on a foil-lined large baking sheet. Roast 20 to 25 minutes or until skins are blistered and dark. Bring foil up around peppers to enclose. Let stand about 15 minutes or until cool. Using a sharp knife, loosen edges of the skins; gently pull off the skin in strips and discard.
2. Meanwhile, in a medium saucepan cook onion and garlic in hot oil over medium about 5 minutes or until tender. Stir in roasted peppers, broth, and sweet potato. Bring to boiling; reduce heat. Cover and simmer 15 minutes. Cool slightly. Stir in the snipped basil and the vinegar.
3. Place half of the pepper mixture in a food processor or blender. Cover and pulse until smooth. Repeat with the remaining pepper mixture. Return all of mixture to saucepan; heat through.
4. To serve, ladle soup into small heatproof glasses (such as shot glasses or cups). Garnish with short skewers or cocktail picks threaded with tomato halves and basil leaves.

To Make Ahead Prepare as directed through Step 3, except do not heat through; let cool. Store in an airtight container in the refrigerator up to

Roasted Pepper Soup Shooters

2 days. To serve, transfer to a medium saucepan and heat over medium-low until heated through, stirring occasionally. Serve as directed.

PER SERVING *(1 shooter each)* **CAL** 80, **FAT** 1 g (0 g sat. fat), **CHOL** 0 mg, **SODIUM** 73 mg, **CARB** 17 g (3 g fiber, 8 g sugars), **PRO** 2 g

Panko Roasted Asparagus

4 g CARB

SERVES 16
HANDS ON 20 min.
TOTAL 32 min.

- 1 lb. thick asparagus spears
- ½ cup mayonnaise
- ¼ cup Dijon-style mustard
- 2 tsp. lemon juice
- 1 cup panko bread crumbs
- 2 Tbsp. peanut oil

1. Preheat oven to 425°F. Snap off and discard woody bases from asparagus. In a small bowl combine mayonnaise, mustard, and lemon juice. Transfer half of the mixture to a serving bowl; cover and chill until ready to serve.
2. Place bread crumbs in a shallow dish. Spread the remaining mayonnaise mixture over asparagus spears; roll in bread crumbs to coat. Arrange coated asparagus in an ungreased 15×10-inch baking pan. Drizzle with oil.
3. Roast about 12 minutes or until bread crumbs are golden brown. Serve asparagus with reserved mayonnaise mixture. If desired, sprinkle with *black pepper*.

PER SERVING *(1 spear each)* **CAL** 88, **FAT** 7 g (1 g sat. fat), **CHOL** 3 mg, **SODIUM** 139 mg, **CARB** 4 g (1 g fiber, 1 g sugars), **PRO** 1 g

**Sage-Embosssed
Fingerling Potatoes**

Avocado-and-Pesto-Stuffed Tomatoes

1g
CARB

SERVES 30
HANDS ON 20 min.
TOTAL 50 min.

- 30 cherry tomatoes (about 2½ cups)
- ½ of an avocado, peeled and cut up
- 2 oz. cream cheese, softened
- 2 Tbsp. basil pesto
- 1 tsp. lemon juice
  Fresh basil leaves (optional)

1. Cut a thin slice from the tops of each tomato. If necessary, cut a thin slice from the bottoms so each stands upright. Using a small spoon or a melon baller, carefully hollow out tomatoes. Invert onto a paper towel-lined baking sheet and let stand 30 minutes to drain.
2. For filling, in a food processor combine avocado, cream cheese, pesto, and lemon juice. Cover and process until smooth. If desired, line a platter with fresh basil leaves. Spoon filling into tomatoes and place on platter.

To Make Ahead Loosely cover stuffed tomatoes with plastic wrap and chill up to 4 hours.

PER SERVING (1 stuffed tomato each) **CAL** 18, **FAT** 1 g (1 g sat. fat), **CHOL** 2 mg, **SODIUM** 16 mg, **CARB** 1 g (0 g fiber, 1 g sugars), **PRO** 0 g

Sage-Embossed Fingerling Potatoes

3g
CARB

SERVES 30
HANDS ON 15 min.
TOTAL 30 min.

- 15 fingerling potatoes and/or small new potatoes
- 2 Tbsp. olive oil
- ¼ tsp. hickory smoked salt or seasoned salt
- 30 fresh sage leaves

1. Preheat oven to 425°F. Line a baking sheet with parchment paper.
2. Cut potatoes in half lengthwise. In a bowl combine potatoes, oil, and salt; toss gently to coat. Press a sage leaf against the cut side of each potato half. Arrange potatoes, cut sides down, on prepared baking sheet.
3. Bake 15 to 20 minutes or until potatoes are tender. Serve warm or at room temperature.

PER SERVING (1 potato half each) **CAL** 19, **FAT** 1 g (0 g sat. fat), **CHOL** 0 mg, **SODIUM** 14 mg, **CARB** 3 g (0 g fiber, 0 g sugars), **PRO** 0 g

Avocado-and-Pesto-Stuffed Tomatoes

Spanish Potato Omelet

Spanish Potato Omelet

5g
CARB

SERVES 16
HANDS ON 20 min.
SLOW COOK 2½ hr.

Nonstick cooking spray
1 lb. russet potatoes, peeled and cut into ¾-inch pieces
2 Tbsp. olive oil
½ cup chopped onion
¾ tsp. salt
¼ tsp. black pepper
12 eggs, lightly beaten
½ cup shredded reduced-fat cheddar cheese (2 oz.)
½ cup chopped tomato

1. Line a 3½- or 4-qt. round slow cooker with a disposable slow cooker liner. Coat the liner with cooking spray. In a 10-inch skillet cook potatoes in hot oil over medium about 5 minutes or until lightly browned, stirring frequently. Add onion; cook 2 to 3 minutes more or until onion is tender, stirring frequently (the potatoes should still be firm).
2. Transfer potato mixture to the prepared slow cooker. Sprinkle with salt and pepper. Pour eggs over potato mixture; stir gently to evenly distribute potatoes. Cover and cook on low about 2½ hours or until eggs are set.
3. Using a knife, loosen omelet from disposable liner; transfer omelet to a plate. Sprinkle with cheese. Cover with foil and let stand 5 minutes to slightly melt cheese. Cut omelet into wedges. Top with tomato. Serve warm or at room temperature.

PER SERVING (1 wedge each) **CAL** 101, **FAT** 6 g (2 g sat. fat), **CHOL** 142 mg, **SODIUM** 195 mg, **CARB** 5 g (1 g fiber, 1 g sugars), **PRO** 6 g

Sweet Onion-Tomato Tartlets

Sweet Onion-Tomato Tartlets

11g
CARB

SERVES 18
HANDS ON 30 min.
TOTAL 1 hr. 15 min.

3 cups grape tomatoes
1 sweet onion, quartered and thinly sliced (about 2 cups)
1 Tbsp. snipped fresh rosemary
1 Tbsp. olive oil
½ tsp. salt
½ tsp. black pepper
1 Tbsp. sherry vinegar
1 17.3-oz. pkg. (2 sheets) frozen puff pastry sheets, thawed
Manchego or Parmigiano-Reggiano cheese, shaved

1. Preheat oven to 400°F. Prick tomatoes with a fork or the tip of a sharp knife. In an ungreased 15×10-inch baking pan combine tomatoes and the next five ingredients (through pepper). Roast 25 to 30 minutes or until onion is tender. Remove from oven. Sprinkle with vinegar; let cool.
2. Meanwhile, line a large baking sheet with parchment paper or foil. On a lightly floured surface unfold puff pastry. Using a 3-inch round cookie cutter, cut pastry into rounds. Place rounds on the prepared baking sheet.
3. Spoon about 2 Tbsp. of the roasted tomato mixture onto each pastry round. Bake 15 to 20 minutes or until edges are puffed and golden brown. Let stand on baking sheet 5 minutes before serving. Top with shaved cheese.

PER SERVING (1 tartlet each) **CAL** 119, **FAT** 8 g (2 g sat. fat), **CHOL** 1 mg, **SODIUM** 117 mg, **CARB** 11 g (1 g fiber, 2 g sugars), **PRO** 2 g

Hot Artichoke-Kale Dip

10 g CARB

SERVES 16
HANDS ON 20 min.
TOTAL 1 hr.

- 1 Tbsp. olive oil
- 1 cup chopped sweet onion
- 3 cloves garlic, minced
- 8 cups torn stemmed kale
- 4 oz. reduced-fat cream cheese (neufchatel), softened
- ⅔ cup plain fat-free Greek yogurt
- ½ cup shredded part-skim mozzarella cheese (2 oz.)
- ¼ cup fat-free milk
- 1 tsp. dried Italian seasoning, crushed
- 2 14-oz. cans artichoke hearts, drained and coarsely chopped
- 3 Tbsp. finely shredded Parmesan cheese (1 oz.)
- 8 cups veggie dippers (sweet pepper strips, carrot and celery sticks, cucumber slices, Belgian endive leaves)

1. Preheat oven to 350°F. In a 12-inch skillet heat oil over medium. Add onion and garlic; cook about 10 minutes or until tender, stirring occasionally. Add kale; toss with tongs 2 to 3 minutes or until wilted.

2. In a bowl stir together the next five ingredients (through Italian seasoning) until well combined. Stir in kale mixture and artichoke hearts. Spoon into 2-qt. square baking dish. Sprinkle Parmesan on top. Bake, covered, about 15 minutes. Uncover and bake about 15 minutes more or until hot and bubbly. Serve with veggie dippers.

PER SERVING (¼ cup each) **CAL** 89, **FAT** 4 g (2 g sat. fat), **CHOL** 9 mg, **SODIUM** 194 mg, **CARB** 10 g (3 g fiber, 4 g sugars), **PRO** 5 g

3

COMFORTING
SOUPS & STEWS

The holidays can be hectic, so sink your spoon into a steaming

bowl of comforting soup or thick chili for a calming effect. Or keep

a pot of stew simmering on the stove on days when the family is

coming and going at different mealtimes. On the big day, serve

small bowls of a creamy soup to begin the holiday meal.

Thick Chicken Chili

Thick Chicken Chili

24 g CARB

SERVES 8
HANDS ON 35 min.
TOTAL 1 hr. 5 min.

- 2 14½-oz. cans no-salt-added diced tomatoes, undrained
- 4 cups reduced-sodium chicken broth
- 2 15-oz. cans no-salt-added cannellini beans, rinsed and drained
- 2 cups ½-inch-thick carrot slices
- 1 cup chopped onion
- 3 Tbsp. chili powder
- ½ tsp. salt
- ½ tsp. crushed red pepper
- 1 Tbsp. canola oil
- 1½ lb. skinless, boneless chicken breast halves, cut into ½- to ¾-inch chunks
  Fat-free sour cream (optional)
  Snipped fresh cilantro (optional)

1. Place tomatoes in a blender or food processor; cover and blend or process until smooth. In a 5- to 6-qt. pot combine tomatoes and the next seven ingredients (through crushed red pepper). Bring to boiling; reduce heat. Simmer, uncovered, about 30 minutes or until carrots are tender and chili is thickened, stirring occasionally.
2. Meanwhile, heat 1½ tsp. of the oil in a 10-inch nonstick skillet over medium-high. Add half of the chicken. Cook and stir 4 to 5 minutes or until chicken is no longer pink. Transfer cooked chicken to a bowl. Repeat with the remaining 1½ tsp. oil and remaining chicken.
3. Stir cooked chicken into the pot; heat through. If desired, top chili with sour cream and/or snipped cilantro.

PER SERVING *(1¼ cups each)* **CAL** 244, **FAT** 5 g (1 g sat. fat), **CHOL** 54 mg, **SODIUM** 642 mg, **CARB** 24 g (8 g fiber, 6 g sugars), **PRO** 26 g

Sausage, Bean, and Kale Soup

36 g CARB

SERVES 8
HANDS ON 30 min.
TOTAL 1 hr. 40 min.

- 6 oz. dried Great Northern beans, rinsed and drained
- 2 Tbsp. olive oil
- 3 smoked chicken sausage links with apple (9 oz.), halved lengthwise and sliced
- ⅓ cup regular pearled barley
- 1½ cups chopped onion
- 1½ cups chopped carrots
- ¾ cup chopped fennel bulb
- 3 cloves garlic, minced
- 2 32-oz. cartons no-salt-added chicken broth
- 1 bay leaf
- 1 Tbsp. snipped fresh thyme leaves
- ½ tsp. salt
- ¼ tsp. black pepper
- 8 cups torn fresh stemmed kale
- 2 Tbsp. red wine vinegar

1. Place beans in a bowl; cover with water. Soak overnight. (Or place beans in a large pot; add water to cover. Bring to boiling. Boil, uncovered, 2 minutes. Remove from heat. Cover and let stand 1 hour.) Drain and rinse beans.
2. In a 6- to 8-qt. Dutch oven heat 1 Tbsp. of the oil over medium-high. Add sausage and barley; cook about 3 minutes or until browned, stirring occasionally. Remove from pan. Add the remaining 1 Tbsp. oil to pan. Add onion, carrots, fennel, and garlic; cook and stir about 6 minutes or until tender. Stir in beans, sausage and barley, and the next five ingredients (through pepper). Bring to boiling; reduce heat. Cover and simmer about 1 hour or until beans are tender, stirring occasionally.
3. Stir in kale. Return to boiling; reduce heat. Cover and simmer 10 minutes. Remove and discard bay leaf. Stir in vinegar.

PER SERVING *(1⅓ cups each)* **CAL** 270, **FAT** 7 g (1 g sat. fat), **CHOL** 23 mg, **SODIUM** 499 mg, **CARB** 36 g (9 g fiber, 9 g sugars), **PRO** 18 g

QUICK TIP Bolster the apple flavor in this soup by sprinkling finely chopped unpeeled fresh apple over the top.

Sausage, Bean, and Kale Soup

Tofu is the hidden ingredient in this creamy soup, and it really amps up the protein. To get the best result, you must use the soft, silken-style variety. Firm tofu does not blend as smoothly.

Creamy Chicken
and Wild Rice Soup

Creamy Chicken and Wild Rice Soup

22 g
CARB

SERVES 8
HANDS ON 30 min.
SLOW COOK 6 hr. 30 min.

- 2 Tbsp. olive oil
- 1½ lb. skinless, boneless chicken thighs
- 2 8-oz. pkg. sliced fresh button mushrooms
- 1 32-oz. carton reduced-sodium chicken broth
- 2 cups water
- 1½ cups thinly sliced leeks
- 1½ cups ½-inch slices celery
- ¾ cup uncooked wild rice, rinsed and drained
- ¾ tsp. salt
- 1 12-oz. pkg. soft, silken-style tofu
- 1 cup low-fat milk (1%)
- ¼ cup all-purpose flour
- 1 Tbsp. fresh thyme leaves

1. In a 12-inch skillet heat oil over medium-high. Add chicken; cook about 6 minutes or until browned, turning once.
2. In a 6-qt. slow cooker combine chicken and the next seven ingredients (through salt). Cover and cook on low 6 hours or high 3 hours. Remove chicken from cooker. Coarsely shred chicken using two forks.
3. If slow cooker is on low, turn to high. In a blender combine the remaining ingredients. Cover and blend until smooth. Stir into mixture in cooker. Cover and cook 30 minutes more or until thick. Stir in shredded chicken.

PER SERVING *(1¾ cups each)* **CAL** 271, **FAT** 9 g (2 g sat. fat), **CHOL** 81 mg, **SODIUM** 601 mg, **CARB** 22 g (2 g fiber, 5 g sugars), **PRO** 26 g

Turkey Tortellini Soup

25 g
CARB

SERVES 6
HANDS ON 25 min.
SLOW COOK 6 hr. 30 min.

- 4 cups reduced-sodium chicken broth
- 4 cups water
- 4 cups coarsely chopped roasted turkey breast (1 lb.)
- 1 14.5-oz. can no-salt-added diced tomatoes, undrained
- 1 Tbsp. dried Italian seasoning, crushed
- 1 9-oz. pkg. refrigerated cheese tortellini
- 2 cups fresh baby spinach
- 6 Tbsp. shredded Parmesan cheese (optional)

1. Place a disposable slow cooker liner in a 5- to 6-qt. slow cooker. Add the first five ingredients (through Italian seasoning).
2. Cover and cook on low 6 to 8 hours or high 3 to 4 hours. If slow cooker is on low, turn to high. Stir in tortellini. Cover and cook about 30 minutes more or until tortellini is tender. Stir in spinach. If desired, sprinkle each serving with 1 Tbsp. Parmesan cheese.

PER SERVING *(2 cups each)* **CAL** 240, **FAT** 3 g (2 g sat. fat), **CHOL** 63 mg, **SODIUM** 656 mg, **CARB** 25 g (3 g fiber, 4 g sugars), **PRO** 28 g

Turkey Tortellini Soup

Turkey Noodle Soup

29 g
CARB

SERVES 6
HANDS ON 15 min.
TOTAL 50 min.

- 6 cups unsalted chicken stock
- 1 14.5-oz. can no-salt-added fire-roasted diced tomatoes, undrained
- 1 16-oz. pkg. frozen mixed vegetables (carrots, peas, corn, green beans, and lima beans)
- ½ cup sliced celery
- ½ cup thin wedges onion
- 2 tsp. Italian seasoning, crushed
- 3 cloves garlic, minced
- ¾ tsp. salt
- ¼ tsp. black pepper
- 4 oz. medium dried egg noodles (2¼ cups)
- 2 cups chopped cooked skinless, boneless turkey breast (12 oz.)
- 1 Tbsp. cider vinegar

1. In a 4- to 6-qt. Dutch oven combine the first nine ingredients (through pepper). Bring to boiling; reduce heat. Simmer, covered, about 30 minutes or until vegetables are tender. Add noodles, turkey, and vinegar. Return to boiling. Cook 5 to 7 minutes or until noodles are tender, stirring occasionally.

PER SERVING *(2 cups each)* **CAL** 250, **FAT** 2 g (1 g sat. fat), **CHOL** 56 mg, **SODIUM** 540 mg, **CARB** 29 g (5 g fiber, 4 g sugars), **PRO** 27 g

Turkey Noodle Soup

Baked Potato Chowder with Bacon-Cheddar Potato Skins

27 g
CARB

SERVES 6
HANDS ON 20 min.
TOTAL 1 hr. 20 min.

- 3 medium (4 to 5 oz. each) Yukon gold potatoes
- 4 slices lower-sodium, less-fat bacon, chopped
- 1 cup chopped carrots
- ½ cup thinly sliced celery
- ½ cup chopped onion
- 3 cloves garlic, minced
- 2 14.5-oz. cans reduced-sodium chicken broth
- 2 cups ½-inch pieces peeled rutabaga or turnips (8 oz.)
- ½ cup shredded reduced-fat cheddar cheese (2 oz.)
- ⅓ cup light sour cream
- 3 Tbsp. snipped fresh chives
- 2 Tbsp. all-purpose flour
- 2½ cups fat-free milk
- 2 cups chopped cooked skinless, boneless chicken breast
  Black pepper (optional)

1. Preheat oven to 425°F. Line a shallow baking pan with foil. Scrub potatoes and prick with a fork; place potatoes on prepared pan. Bake 45 to 55 minutes or until tender; let cool.
2. Meanwhile, in a 4-qt. Dutch oven cook bacon over medium until browned and crisp, stirring occasionally. Using a slotted spoon, transfer bacon to paper towels. Discard all but 2 teaspoons drippings in pot. Add carrots, celery, and onion. Cook over medium 5 minutes, stirring occasionally. Add garlic; cook and stir 1 minute more. Add broth and rutabaga. Bring to boiling; reduce heat. Simmer, uncovered, 10 to 12 minutes or until rutabaga is tender.
3. Cut cooled potatoes lengthwise in half. Using a spoon, scoop out the flesh from each potato half and place in a large bowl, leaving a ¼-inch-thick potato skin.

4. Increase oven temperature to 450°F. Place potato skins, skin sides down, in the same baking pan. Sprinkle with the cheese and half of the cooked bacon. Bake 5 to 7 minutes or until cheese is melted and potato skins are heated through. Top with sour cream and sprinkle with half the chives.
5. Mash the reserved potato flesh. Stir in the flour. Gradually stir in milk until mixture is nearly smooth. Add potato mixture to soup. Cook, stirring occasionally, until thickened and bubbly. Add the chicken and remaining bacon. Cook and stir 5 minutes more or until heated.
6. Sprinkle soup with remaining chives and, if desired, pepper. Serve with potato skins.

PER SERVING *(1½ cups soup + 1 potato skin each)* **CAL** 279, **FAT** 7 g (3 g sat. fat), **CHOL** 56 mg, **SODIUM** 559 mg, **CARB** 27 g (3 g fiber, 10 g sugars), **PRO** 26 g

Baked Potato Chowder with Bacon-Cheddar Potato Skins

Porcini Meatball Soup with Swiss Chard Ribbons

10 g **CARB**

SERVES 6
HANDS ON 25 min.
SLOW COOK 8 hr. 15 min.

- 1 oz. dried porcini mushrooms
- 2 cups boiling water
- 1 egg, lightly beaten
- ½ cup soft bread crumbs
- ½ cup finely chopped onion
- ½ cup grated Parmesan cheese
- ¼ cup milk
- 1 tsp. dried oregano, crushed
- ½ tsp. salt
- 1 clove garlic, minced
- 12 oz. lean ground beef or uncooked ground turkey
- 1 14.5-oz. can reduced-sodium chicken broth
- 1 14.5-oz. can no-salt-added diced tomatoes, undrained
- ½ cup finely chopped celery
- 1 bunch Swiss chard, stems removed and chopped or thinly sliced (about 8 cups)

1. Preheat oven to 375°F. Line a shallow baking pan with parchment paper. Place dried mushrooms in a medium bowl; pour boiling water over mushrooms. Cover and let stand 15 minutes. Using a slotted spoon, remove mushrooms, reserving liquid. Finely chop mushrooms.

2. For meatballs, in another medium bowl combine egg, bread crumbs, ¼ cup of the onion, ¼ cup of the cheese, the milk, oregano, salt, garlic, and chopped mushrooms. Add ground beef; mix well. Form mixture into thirty 1-inch meatballs. Place meatballs in the prepared baking pan. Bake about 10 minutes or until meatballs are browned. Using a slotted spoon, transfer meatballs to paper towels.

3. Slowly pour all but about ¼ cup of the reserved mushroom liquid (discard liquid at bottom of bowl, which may be gritty) into a 3½- or 4-qt. slow cooker. Stir in broth, tomatoes, celery, and the remaining ¼ cup onion. Carefully transfer meatballs to mixture in cooker. Cover and cook on low 8 to 10 hours or on high 4 to 5 hours.

4. If slow cooker is on low, turn to high. Stir in Swiss chard. Cover and cook 15 minutes more. Top with the remaining ¼ cup cheese.

Tip If desired, cover and chill meatballs and the reserved mushroom liquid separately up to 24 hours.

PER SERVING *(1⅓ cups each)* **CAL** 196, **FAT** 9 g (4 g sat. fat), **CHOL** 75 mg, **SODIUM** 663 mg, **CARB** 10 g (2 g fiber, 5 g sugars), **PRO** 19 g

Porcini Meatball Soup with Swiss Chard Ribbons

Sweets and Sour Beef Stew

21 g **CARB**

SERVES 8
HANDS ON 30 min.
TOTAL 1 hr. 55 min.

- 2 Tbsp. canola oil
- 1 to 1¼ lb. beef flank steak, trimmed, cut into ¾-inch cubes
- 1 32-oz. carton 50%-less-sodium beef broth
- 1 14.5-oz. can no-salt-added diced tomatoes, undrained
- 1 cup water
- ¾ cup chopped onion
- 2 tsp. sweet paprika
- 1 tsp. caraway seeds, crushed
- ½ tsp. salt
- ¼ tsp. black pepper
- 1 lb. sweet potatoes, peeled and cut into ¾-inch pieces (3 cups)
- 3 cups chopped bok choy
- 1 cup chopped red sweet pepper
- 1 Tbsp. honey
- 2 Tbsp. balsamic vinegar

Sweets and Sour Beef Stew

1. In a 6-qt. Dutch oven heat oil over medium-high. Brown beef, half at a time, stirring occasionally. Return all beef to Dutch oven.
2. Stir in the next eight ingredients (through black pepper). Bring to boiling; reduce heat. Cover and simmer 1 to 1¼ hours or until meat is nearly tender.
3. Stir in sweet potatoes, bok choy, sweet pepper, and honey. Simmer about 15 minutes or until potatoes are tender. Stir in vinegar just before serving.

PER SERVING (1½ cups each) **CAL** 206, **FAT** 7 g (1 g sat. fat), **CHOL** 35 mg, **SODIUM** 449 mg, **CARB** 21 g (4 g fiber, 9 g sugars), **PRO** 15 g

Spicy Ancho Beef Stew

Pork, Spinach, and Rice Soup

25 g
CARB

SERVES 6
HANDS ON 25 min.
TOTAL 55 min.

- 2 Tbsp. canola oil
- 1 to 1¼ lb. pork tenderloin, trimmed and cut into bite-size pieces
- 8 oz. fresh sliced mushrooms
- 1 cup coarsely chopped onion
- 2 cloves garlic, minced
- 4 cups no-salt-added vegetable broth
- 2 cups cooked brown rice
- ½ tsp. salt
- ½ tsp. crushed red pepper
- 2 5-oz. pkg. fresh spinach, coarsely chopped
- 3 oz. shredded Parmesan cheese

1. Preheat oven to 350°F. Heat 1 Tbsp. of the oil in a Dutch oven over medium-high. Cook pork in hot oil about 5 minutes or until browned on all sides. Remove pork from pan; keep warm.
2. Add the remaining 1 Tbsp. of the oil to the Dutch oven. Add mushrooms, onion, and garlic. Cook and stir until onions are tender, scraping up the browned bits on the bottom of the pan.
3. Stir in the broth, rice, salt, and crushed red pepper. Bring to boiling, reduce heat. Simmer, uncovered, 10 minutes. Stir in spinach and browned pork. Cook and stir until spinach is wilted and pork is cooked through.
4. Meanwhile, line a large baking sheet with parchment paper. For Parmesan crisps, spoon Parmesan cheese into six mounds (2 Tbsp. each), spacing mounds at least 2 inches apart. Using the back of a spoon, carefully pat each mound into a 3-inch circle. Bake 10 to 12 minutes or until golden brown. Let crisps cool on baking sheet.
5. Serve soup with Parmesan crisps.

PER SERVING *(1⅓ cups + 1 crisp each)*
CAL 303, **FAT** 11 g (4 g sat. fat), **CHOL** 59 mg, **SODIUM** 607 mg, **CARB** 25 g (4 g fiber, 4 g sugars), **PRO** 26 g

Spicy Ancho Beef Stew

32 g
CARB

SERVES 8
HANDS ON 25 min.
TOTAL 4 hr. 25 min.

- 1½ lb. beef stew meat
- ½ tsp. salt
- 8 oz. uncooked chorizo sausage or other sausage, casings removed
- ½ cup chopped onion
- 4 cloves garlic, minced
- ½ cup all-purpose flour
- 2 tsp. ground ancho chile pepper
- 2 tsp. Mexican-style chili powder or chili powder
- 1 12-oz. bottle dark Mexican beer, such as Negra Modelo
- 1 14.5-oz. can no-salt-added diced tomatoes, undrained
- 2 lb. Yukon gold potatoes, cut into ½-inch pieces
- 2 large carrots, peeled and cut into ½-inch pieces

1. Preheat oven to 300°F. Sprinkle stew meat with salt. In a 5- to 6-qt. Dutch oven cook the sausage over medium-high until browned. Transfer sausage to a bowl using a slotted spoon. Add stew meat in batches to pan and sear about 5 minutes per side or until deep brown all over. Transfer stew meat to bowl with sausage.
2. Add onion to pot; cook and stir about 4 minutes or until lightly browned. Add garlic; cook and stir 1 minute. Stir in flour, ground ancho chile pepper, and chili powder; cook and stir 1 minute. Stir in beer and tomatoes. Bring to boiling; reduce heat. Simmer, uncovered, 1 minute. Return sausage and beef to pot. Stir in potatoes and carrots. Add just enough water to cover vegetables (about 2 cups).
3. Return to boiling. Cover and bake 4 hours or until vegetables and meat are fork-tender. Skim off any surface fat before serving.

PER SERVING *(1½ cups each)* **CAL** 359, **FAT** 12 g (5 sat. fat), **CHOL** 73 mg, **SODIUM** 550 mg, **CARB** 32 g (5 g fiber, 4 g sugars), **PRO** 27 g

QUICK TIP Enjoy two crisps per serving by using 1 tablespoon cheese each, then bake a little less.

Pork, Spinach, and Rice Soup

Cider Pork and Apple Stew

**Pumpkin-Kale
Calico Bean Stew**

Cider Pork and Apple Stew

24 g
CARB

SERVES 8

HANDS ON 50 min.

TOTAL 2 hr. 50 min.

- 2 lb. boneless pork shoulder, cut into 1-inch pieces
- ½ tsp. salt
- 1 Tbsp. vegetable oil
- 3 parsnips and/or carrots, peeled and sliced
- 1 small red onion, halved and sliced
- 1 Tbsp. snipped fresh sage
- 1 Tbsp. minced fresh ginger
- 4 cloves garlic, minced
- 5 Granny Smith apples, cored and cut into 1-inch pieces
- 4 cups reduced-sodium chicken broth
- 1 cup apple cider or juice
- 3 Tbsp. cider vinegar
- 2 Tbsp. apple brandy (optional)
  Sour cream (optional)
  Freshly grated nutmeg
  and/or cracked black pepper
  (optional)

1. Preheat oven to 300°F. Season pork with salt. In a 4-qt. Dutch oven heat oil over medium-high. Add pork, in batches, and cook 6 to 8 minutes or until browned all over. Transfer pork to a bowl. Add parsnips and onion to pot; cook and stir 4 minutes. Transfer vegetables to bowl with pork. Add sage, ginger, and garlic to pot; cook and stir 1 minute. Add three of the apples, the broth, cider, and vinegar to pot. Bring to boiling; reduce heat. Simmer, covered, about 5 minutes or until apples are tender. Puree mixture with an immersion blender or transfer, in batches, to a blender and blend until smooth. Add pork, parsnips, and onion. Bring to boiling.
2. Cover; bake about 2 hours or until pork is fork tender. Stir in remaining apples and, if desired, brandy. If desired, top with sour cream, nutmeg, pepper, and/or additional sage.

PER SERVING *(1⅓ cups each)* **CAL** 272, **FAT** 8 g *(2 g sat. fat)*, **CHOL** 68 mg, **SODIUM** 504 mg, **CARB** 24 g *(4 g fiber, 15 g sugars)*, **PRO** 24 g

Pumpkin-Kale Calico Bean Stew

52 g
CARB

SERVES 6

HANDS ON 30 min.

SLOW COOK 11 hr. 30 min.

- ½ cup dried Great Northern beans
- ½ cup dried pinto beans
- ½ cup dried black beans
- 4 cups unsalted vegetable stock
- 1 15-oz. can pumpkin
- 1 cup chopped onion
- 1½ tsp. ground cumin
- 1 tsp. dried oregano, crushed
- 1 tsp. chili powder
- ½ tsp. salt
- 4 cups roughly chopped fresh kale
- 1 14.5-oz. can Italian-style stewed tomatoes, undrained and cut up
- 1 cup frozen shelled edamame, thawed
- 1 Tbsp. Louisiana hot sauce

1. Rinse beans; drain. In a large saucepan combine beans and enough water to cover beans by 2 inches. Bring to boiling; reduce heat. Simmer, uncovered, 10 minutes. Remove from heat. Cover and let stand 1 hour. Drain and rinse beans.
2. In a 4-qt. slow cooker combine beans and the next seven ingredients (through salt).
3. Cover and cook on low 11 to 12 hours or high 5 ½ to 6 hours. If slow cooker is on low, turn to high. Stir in the remaining ingredients. Cover and cook 30 minutes more.

Tip For easy cleanup, line slow cooker with a disposable slow cooker liner. After removing food from slow cooker, dispose of the liner. Do not lift or transport the liner with food inside.

PER SERVING *(1½ cups each)* **CAL** 286, **FAT** 3 g *(0 g sat. fat)*, **CHOL** 0 mg, **SODIUM** 597 mg, **CARB** 52 g *(14 g fiber, 13 g sugars)*, **PRO** 17 g

Pumpkin Spice
Butternut Squash Soup

Roasted Red Pepper Soup

16 g
CARB

SERVES 4
TOTAL 20 min.

2 12-oz. jars roasted red
   peppers, drained and cut up
   (2⅓ cups total)
1 cup unsalted chicken or
   vegetable stock
⅓ cup chopped onion
1 clove garlic, minced
½ tsp. dried thyme, crushed
¼ tsp. salt
¼ tsp. black pepper
1 12-oz. pkg. silken soft tofu
1 cup low-fat milk (1%)
¼ cup plain fat-free Greek yogurt
¼ cup dry-roasted unsalted
   sunflower kernels

1. In a medium saucepan combine the
first seven ingredients (through black
pepper). Bring to boiling; reduce heat.
Simmer, covered, 10 minutes. Remove
from heat.
2. Transfer soup to a blender or food
processor. Add tofu and milk. Cover
and blend or process until smooth.
Return soup to saucepan; heat
through.
3. Top each serving of soup with
1 Tbsp. each of the yogurt and
sunflower kernels. Serve immediately.

PER SERVING *(about 1 cup each)* **CAL** 226,
FAT 10 g (2 g sat. fat), **CHOL** 3 mg,
SODIUM 526 mg, **CARB** 16 g (3 g fiber,
8 g sugars), **PRO** 17 g

**Roasted
Red Pepper
Soup**

Pumpkin Spice
Butternut Squash Soup

16 g
CARB

SERVES 12
HANDS ON 40 min.
TOTAL 1 hr.

1 Tbsp. olive oil
⅓ cup chopped onion
2 cloves garlic, minced
8 cups peeled and cubed
   butternut squash
⅔ cup chopped apple
½ cup chopped carrot
¾ tsp. kosher salt
½ tsp. pumpkin pie spice
¼ tsp. black pepper
1 14.5-oz. can reduced-sodium
   chicken broth
1 14-oz. can unsweetened light
   coconut milk
1 Tbsp. packed brown sugar*
5 Tbsp. plain fat-free Greek
   yogurt
5 Tbsp. salted, roasted pumpkin
   seeds (pepitas)

1. In a 4- to 6-qt. Dutch oven heat oil
over medium. Add onion and garlic;
cook 5 minutes or until onion is tender,
stirring occasionally. Stir in the next six
ingredients (through pepper). Cook
and stir 4 minutes. Add broth. Bring to
boiling; reduce heat. Simmer, covered,
20 to 25 minutes or until squash and
carrot are tender, stirring occasionally.
Remove from heat. Stir in coconut milk
and brown sugar.
2. Using an immersion blender (or
working in batches in a food processor
or blender), blend squash mixture until
smooth, adding water if needed to
reach desired consistency.
3. Serve soup topped with yogurt,
pumpkin seeds, and, if desired,
additional pumpkin pie spice.

PER SERVING *(⅔ cup each)* **CAL** 131,
FAT 6 g (3 g sat. fat), **CHOL** 0 mg,
SODIUM 133 mg, **CARB** 16 g (3 g fiber,
5 g sugars), **PRO** 4 g

*Sugar Sub Choose Splenda Brown
Sugar Blend. Follow package
directions to use 1 Tbsp. equivalent.

PER SERVING WITH SUB Same as above,
except **CAL** 129, **SUGARS** 4 g

Chickpea, Leek, and Spinach Soup

37 g
CARB

SERVES 4
TOTAL 25 min.

- 2 Tbsp. olive oil
- 2 medium leeks, white and light green parts only, thinly sliced, washed, and drained
- 2 15- to 16-oz. cans chickpeas (garbanzo beans), rinsed and drained
- 2 cloves garlic, thinly sliced
- 4 cups no-salt-added chicken or vegetable broth
- 1 cup water
- 3 Tbsp. fresh lemon juice
- 2 5-oz. pkg. fresh baby spinach
- 1 Tbsp. fresh thyme, chopped
- ¼ tsp. salt
- ¼ tsp. black pepper

1. In a 4 qt. Dutch oven heat oil over medium heat. Add leeks; cook 5 to 7 minutes or until very tender but not browned, stirring occasionally (reduce heat if leeks begin to brown). Stir in chickpeas and garlic. Cook about 2 minutes more, stirring occasionally.

2. Add broth and the water. Bring to boiling; reduce heat. Add lemon juice. Simmer, uncovered, 5 minutes. Gradually stir in spinach and thyme. Cook until spinach is wilted, about 1 minute. Stir in salt and pepper. Serve immediately.

PER SERVING (2 cups each) **CAL** 281, **FAT** 10 g (1 g sat. fat), **CHOL** 0 mg, **SODIUM** 497 mg, **CARB** 37 g (10 g fiber, 7 g sugars), **PRO** 13 g

4

MAIN-DISH
MASTERPIECES

Holiday meals are meant for entertaining and serving special main

dishes for a crowd, such as a beautiful whole-chicken platter and

a spectacular roasted beef tenderloin. But easy and delicious fixes,

like sheet-pan dinners and veggie-loaded salads, will help to keep

you on a healthful track during the busy times.

Mushroom and Thyme Beef Tenderloin

18g CARB

SERVES 8
HANDS ON 25 min.
TOTAL 10 hr. 15 min.

- 1 cup mushroom broth
- 1 0.75-oz. pkg. dried porcini mushrooms
- ¼ cup dry red wine
- 2 Tbsp. snipped fresh thyme
- 1½ tsp. salt
- 1 tsp. Dijon-style mustard
- ¾ tsp. black pepper
- 1 2½- to 3-lb. beef tenderloin roast
- 1½ lb. carrots, halved lengthwise and, if desired, cut into 3-inch lengths
- 1 lb. cipollini onions, peeled
- 1 lb. fresh button mushrooms, quartered
- 2 Tbsp. olive oil

1. For marinade, in a small saucepan bring mushroom broth to boiling; remove from heat. Stir in dried mushrooms. Cover and let stand 20 minutes. Stir in wine, 1 Tbsp. of the thyme, ½ tsp. of the salt, the mustard, and ¼ tsp. of the pepper; cool.

2. Place meat in a resealable plastic bag set in a shallow dish. Pour marinade over meat. Seal bag; turn to coat meat. Marinate in the refrigerator 8 to 24 hours, turning bag occasionally.

3. Meanwhile, in an extra-large bowl combine carrots, onions, button mushrooms, oil, and the remaining 1 Tbsp. thyme. Cover and chill up to 24 hours.

4. Preheat oven to 425°F. Line an extra-large shallow roasting pan with foil; place a rack on foil. Drain meat, discarding marinade. Place meat on rack in pan. Arrange vegetables around meat. Sprinkle meat and vegetables with the remaining 1 tsp. salt and ½ tsp. pepper.

5. Insert an oven-going meat thermometer into center of meat. Roast about 1¼ hours or until thermometer registers 135°F for medium rare.

6. Transfer meat to a cutting board, reserving pan juices. Cover meat with foil; let stand 15 minutes before slicing (temperature of the meat will rise during standing). Serve with roasted vegetables and the reserved juices.

Tip To peel the onions easily, cut an "X" in the root end of each bulb. Place the onions in boiling water 15 seconds, then transfer to cold water. Remove peels.

PER SERVING *(4 oz. cooked meat + 1 cup vegetables each)* **CAL** 311, **FAT** 12 g (3 g sat. fat), **CHOL** 86 mg, **SODIUM** 469 mg, **CARB** 18 g (3 g fiber, 7 g sugars), **PRO** 35 g

Beef Medallions with Horseradish Sauce, Celery, and Mushrooms

9 g CARB | SERVES 4
TOTAL 35 min.

- 4 5-oz. beef shoulder petite tenders or beef tenderloin steaks, cut 1 inch thick
- ½ tsp. Montreal steak seasoning Nonstick cooking spray
- ½ cup fat-free plain Greek yogurt
- 1 Tbsp. prepared horseradish
- 1 Tbsp. olive oil
- 1 clove garlic, minced
- 8 oz. fresh Brussels sprouts, trimmed and sliced
- ¾ cup celery, cut into ¼-inch diagonal slices
- ⅛ tsp. salt
- 3 cups sliced fresh button mushrooms
- 2 Tbsp. chopped walnuts, toasted
- 1 Tbsp. chopped fresh Italian parsley

1. Sprinkle meat with steak seasoning. Coat a grill pan with cooking spray. Heat pan over medium. Add beef to grill pan and cook 10 to 12 minutes for medium rare (145°F), turning once.
2. For the sauce, in a bowl whisk together the yogurt and horseradish.
3. Meanwhile, in a 10-inch skillet heat oil over medium-high. Add garlic; cook and stir 30 seconds. Add Brussels sprouts, celery, and salt; cook and stir 2 minutes. Add mushrooms; cook and stir 2 to 3 minutes more or until celery is crisp-tender.
4. Spoon vegetable mixture onto plates. Slice steak, if desired, and place on vegetables. Top with horseradish sauce, walnuts, and chopped parsley.

PER SERVING *(1 steak + ⅔ cup vegetables + 2 Tbsp. sauce + 1½ tsp. walnuts each)* **CAL** 310, **FAT** 14 g (3 g sat. fat), **CHOL** 80 mg, **SODIUM** 286 mg, **CARB** 9 g (3 g fiber, 4 g sugars), **PRO** 36 g

Meatballs, Greens, and Orecchiette

32 g CARB | SERVES 6
HANDS ON 45 min.
TOTAL 1 hr.

- 1 recipe Veggie-Full Meatballs
- 1¾ cups dried orecchiette pasta
- 3 Tbsp. olive oil
- 1 8-oz. pkg. button or cremini mushrooms, sliced
- 1 cup sliced zucchini
- ¾ cup chopped red sweet pepper
- 3 cloves garlic, minced
- 8 cups chopped Swiss chard, beet greens, arugula, and/or spinach
- 2 Tbsp. balsamic vinegar
- ¼ cup chopped fresh basil and/or Italian parsley
- ⅛ tsp. salt
- ⅛ tsp. black pepper Grated Parmesan cheese (optional)

1. Prepare Veggie-Full Meatballs. Meanwhile, cook orecchiette according to package directions; drain, reserving some of the pasta water.
2. In a 12-inch skillet or wok heat 1 Tbsp. of the olive oil over medium-high. Add mushrooms, zucchini, and sweet pepper; cook and stir about 6 minutes or until vegetables are tender and any liquid has evaporated. Stir in garlic.
3. Add 1 Tbsp. of the oil to the skillet. Add Swiss chard, in batches, cooking and stirring until chard is wilted. Add the remaining 1 Tbsp. oil, the balsamic vinegar, and orecchiette. Toss to combine. Add enough pasta water to reach desired consistency. Stir in basil, salt, and black pepper. Stir in meatballs. If desired, top with Parmesan.

Veggie-Full Meatballs Preheat oven to 450°F. Line a 15×10-inch baking pan with foil; coat with nonstick cooking spray. In a large bowl stir together 1 lightly beaten egg, ¼ cup unsweetened applesauce, ½ cup

Beef Medallions with Horseradish Sauce, Celery, and Mushrooms

Meatballs, Greens, and Orecchiette

shredded zucchini, ¼ cup finely chopped onion, and ½ tsp. each salt and dried Italian seasoning. Stir in ½ cup soft whole wheat bread crumbs. Add 1 lb. lean ground beef or ground turkey; mix well. Shape meat mixture into 1-inch meatballs. Place in pan; bake about 15 minutes or until cooked through (160°F for beef or 165°F for turkey), turning once.

PER SERVING (*8 meatballs + 1 cup pasta mixture each*) **CAL** 344, **FAT** 14 g (3 g sat. fat), **CHOL** 79 mg, **SODIUM** 476 mg, **CARB** 32 g (3 g fiber, 6 g sugars), **PRO** 23 g

Stout-Braised
Beef Pot Roast

Stout-Braised Beef Pot Roast

33 g
CARB

SERVES 8
HANDS ON 20 min.
TOTAL 3 hr.

1 2- to 2½-lb. boneless beef chuck shoulder pot roast
2 tsp. onion powder
1 tsp. kosher salt
1 tsp. black pepper
1 Tbsp. olive oil
1 cup 50%-less-sodium beef broth
2 Tbsp. all-purpose flour
1 12-oz. bottle Guinness stout or other dark beer
2 Tbsp. minced garlic
1 Tbsp. Worcestershire sauce
3 Tbsp. tomato paste
8 carrots, halved lengthwise and cut into 3-inch chunks
1 8-oz. pkg. whole button mushrooms, any large mushrooms halved
2 medium fennel bulbs, cored and cut into wedges
2 cups frozen pearl onions
8 1-oz. slices artisan-style rye bread

1. Preheat oven to 325°F. Trim fat from meat. Sprinkle meat with onion powder, salt, and pepper.
2. In an ovenproof 6- to 8-qt. Dutch oven heat oil over medium-high. Brown meat on all sides. Remove meat from Dutch oven.
3. In a small bowl whisk together beef broth and flour until combined. Pour mixture into Dutch oven. Gradually whisk in beer, garlic, and Worcestershire sauce until smooth, stirring to scrape up browned bits from the bottom of pan. Add tomato paste; whisk until smooth. Return meat to the Dutch oven. Bring to boiling; cover.
4. Place Dutch oven in oven. Bake 1 hour. Turn roast over and add carrots, mushrooms, fennel, and onions. Bake, covered, about 2 hours more or until the meat is fork-tender and vegetables are tender. Transfer meat and vegetables to a platter; cut or pull meat into chunks. Bring sauce to a gentle boil over medium-high; reduce heat. Simmer, uncovered, 10 minutes. Skim off excess fat. Serve with meat, vegetables, and bread.

PER SERVING *(3 oz. meat + 1 cup vegetables + 6 Tbsp. sauce each)* **CAL** 306, **FAT** 8 g (3 g sat. fat), **CHOL** 64 mg, **SODIUM** 534 mg, **CARB** 33 g (5 g fiber, 8 g sugars), **PRO** 25 g

Spicy Cornmeal-Crusted Chicken with Garlic Spinach

Spicy Cornmeal-Crusted Chicken with Garlic Spinach

19 g
CARB

SERVES 4
HANDS ON 15 min.
TOTAL 50 min..

3 Tbsp. all-purpose flour
2 Tbsp. packaged corn muffin mix
2 tsp. chili powder
½ tsp. Italian seasoning, crushed
½ tsp. black pepper
4 tsp. butter, melted
4 5-oz. skinless, boneless chicken breast halves
1 Tbsp. canola oil
2 cups thinly sliced onions
4 cloves garlic, minced
2 10-oz. pkg. fresh spinach
½ tsp. salt

1. Preheat oven to 375°F. In a shallow dish combine flour, corn muffin mix, chili powder, Italian seasoning, and ¼ tsp. of the pepper. Place melted butter in another shallow dish.
2. Dip chicken in melted butter; turn to coat. Dip in corn muffin mixture; turn to coat evenly. Shake off any excess corn muffin mixture.
3. In a 10-inch nonstick skillet heat 1½ tsp. of the oil over medium-high. Add chicken; cook about 8 minutes or until browned, turning once.
4. Place chicken on a rack placed in a shallow baking pan. Bake, uncovered, 10 to 12 minutes or until done (165°F). Cut into ½-inch-thick slices.
5. Meanwhile, in a 6-qt. Dutch oven heat the remaining 1½ tsp. oil over medium-low. Stir in onion and garlic. Cook, covered, 13 to 15 minutes or until onions are tender, stirring occasionally. Uncover; cook and stir over medium-high 3 to 5 minutes or until golden. Add spinach, salt, and the remaining ¼ tsp. pepper; cook and stir just until wilted. Serve with chicken.

PER SERVING *(4 oz. cooked chicken + 1 cup spinach each)* **CAL** 332, **FAT** 15 g (4 g sat. fat), **CHOL** 77 mg, **SODIUM** 515 mg, **CARB** 19 g (5 g fiber, 4 g sugars), **PRO** 29 g

Chicken Thighs with
Caramelized Onion
and Bacon Dressing

next five ingredients (through pepper). Stir gently to combine. Divide dressing mixture among four individual 12- to 14-oz. casserole dishes.

3. In the same skillet brown the chicken in hot oil over medium about 5 minutes, turning once. Place one chicken thigh on dressing mixture in each casserole. Bake, uncovered, 15 to 20 minutes or until chicken is done (175°F). Before serving, sprinkle with additional snipped fresh parsley.

Tip To dry bread cubes, spread them in an even layer in a 15×10-inch baking pan. Bake in a 300°F oven 10 to 15 minutes or until cubes are dry, stirring twice; cool. (Cubes will continue to dry and crisp as they cool.) Or let bread cubes stand, loosely covered, at room temperature 8 to 12 hours.

PER SERVING (1 casserole each) **CAL** 256, **FAT** 8 g (2 g sat. fat), **CHOL** 82 mg, **SODIUM** 337 mg, **CARB** 21 g (3 g fiber, 5 g sugars), **PRO** 23 g

Chicken Thighs with Caramelized Onion and Bacon Dressing

21 g
CARB

| SERVES 4 |
| HANDS ON 40 min. |
| TOTAL 1 hr. |

- 3 slices lower-sodium, less-fat bacon
- 3 large onions, halved and sliced (3 cups)
- 2 cups cubed multigrain ciabatta rolls (½-inch cubes), dried
- ½ cup reduced-sodium chicken broth
- ¼ cup refrigerated or frozen egg product, thawed, or 1 egg, lightly beaten
- 2 Tbsp. snipped fresh parsley
- ¼ tsp. black pepper
- 4 medium skinless, boneless chicken thighs (about 12 oz.)
- 1 Tbsp. olive oil

1. Preheat oven to 400°F. Heat a 10-inch skillet over medium. Cook bacon in hot skillet about 10 minutes or until brown and crispy, turning once. Drain bacon on paper towels. Reserve 1 Tbsp. of the bacon drippings in skillet. Add onions. Reduce heat to medium-low. Cook, covered, 13 to 15 minutes or until onions are tender, stirring occasionally. Uncover; cook and stir over medium-high 3 to 5 minutes or until golden. Remove from heat.
2. Chop the bacon. In a bowl combine bacon, caramelized onions, and the

Rosemary Roasted Chicken with Tangerine-Walnut Bulgur Pilaf

31 g
CARB

| SERVES 6 |
| HANDS ON 20 min. |
| TOTAL 1 hr. 45 min. |

- 4 cloves garlic, minced
- 1 Tbsp. snipped fresh rosemary
- ½ tsp. salt
- ½ tsp. black pepper
- 1 3½- to 4-lb. broiler-fryer chicken
- 1 recipe Tangerine-Walnut Bulgur Pilaf

1. Preheat oven to 375°F. In a small bowl stir together garlic, rosemary, salt, and pepper. Rinse chicken body cavity; pat dry with paper towels. Using kitchen shears, cut the skin along the side of the breast, cutting along the full length of each side of the breast. Use your fingers to gently loosen and pull the skin away from the breast meat, leaving the skin attached at the top end of the breast and exposing the meat. Use your fingers to loosen the skin from the top of each drumstick and thigh. Rub the breast meat evenly with some of the garlic mixture. Rub the remaining garlic mixture evenly under the skin and on top of the drumstick and thigh meat. Lay the skin of the breast back down over the seasonings and meat.

2. Skewer neck skin of chicken to back; tie legs to tail. Twist wing tips under back. Place chicken, breast side up, on a rack in a shallow roasting pan. If desired, insert a meat thermometer into center of an inside thigh muscle, not touching bone.

3. Roast, uncovered, 45 minutes. Cut string that ties the legs together. Roast 30 to 45 minutes more or until at least 170°F in the thigh. Remove from oven. Cover; let stand 10 minutes before carving.

4. Remove skin from chicken before serving. Serve with Tangerine-Walnut Bulgur Pilaf.

Tangerine-Walnut Bulgur Pilaf
Juice 1 tangerine. Peel, seed, and section 2 more tangerines. In a 10-inch skillet cook 4 cups coarsely chopped, trimmed fresh kale or Swiss chard and ½ cup chopped onion in 1 Tbsp. hot oil over medium 5 minutes, stirring occasionally. Add 1 cup uncooked bulgur. Cook and stir 2 minutes more. Add 1½ cups reduced-sodium chicken broth and ¼ tsp. salt; bring to boiling. Cover and remove from heat. Let stand 15 to 20 minutes or until bulgur is tender and liquid is absorbed. Fluff with a fork. Just before serving, gently stir in tangerine sections, tangerine juice, and ⅓ cup chopped toasted walnuts.

PER SERVING *(4 oz. chicken + ⅔ cup pilaf each)* **CAL** 351, **FAT** 11 g (2 g sat. fat), **CHOL** 89 mg, **SODIUM** 531 mg, **CARB** 31 g (7 g fiber, 7 g sugars), **PRO** 34 g

Rosemary Roasted Chicken with Tangerine-Walnut Bulgur Pilaf

QUICK TIP Make the bulgur pilaf through cooking; cover and chill up to 24 hours. Reheat and add tangerines, juice, and walnuts.

Roasted Chicken
with Root Vegetables

Roasted Chicken with Root Vegetables

26 g CARB

SERVES 8
HANDS ON 55 min.
TOTAL 2 hr. 50 min.

- 1 5-lb. whole chicken, neck and giblets removed and excess fat trimmed
- 1 to 2 lemons
- 2 Tbsp. snipped fresh thyme or 2 tsp. dried thyme, crushed
- 1 Tbsp. light butter with canola oil
- 2 tsp. snipped fresh rosemary or ½ tsp. dried rosemary, crushed
- 4 cloves garlic, minced
- 1 tsp. kosher salt
- ½ tsp. freshly ground black pepper
  Nonstick cooking spray
- 4 medium red, fingerling, or purple potatoes, cut into 1-inch wedges
- 6 large carrots, cut into thirds and thick pieces halved lengthwise
- 1 medium red onion, cut into 1-inch wedges
- 1 Tbsp. olive oil
- 1 Tbsp. coarsely snipped fresh thyme
- 1 tsp. coarsely snipped fresh rosemary
- ¼ tsp. kosher salt
- 6 sprigs fresh thyme
- 1 sprig fresh rosemary, cut into 1-inch pieces

1. Rinse chicken body cavity; pat dry with paper towels. Let chicken stand at room temperature 30 minutes.

2. Place one oven rack in center of oven. Place a second oven rack in bottom third of oven. Preheat oven to 450°F. Line a roasting pan with foil; place a rack in the prepared pan. Remove zest and squeeze juice from one of the lemons; set juice aside. In a small bowl combine lemon zest and the next four ingredients (through garlic). Slip your fingers under breast and leg skin to create pockets. Rub herb mixture over meat in pockets and inside body cavity. Sprinkle chicken and cavity with kosher salt and ¼ tsp. of the pepper. Truss chicken (steps, *right*). Insert a thermometer into center of one of the inside thigh muscles not touching bone.

3. Place chicken, breast side up, on rack in the prepared pan; place pan on middle oven rack. Roast 55 minutes.

4. Meanwhile, line a 15×10-inch baking pan with foil and coat with cooking spray. In a large bowl combine the next seven ingredients (though ¼ tsp. salt) and remaining ¼ tsp. pepper. Spread vegetables in prepared pan. Top with thyme and rosemary sprigs.

5. After the chicken has roasted 55 minutes, place vegetables on bottom oven rack. Roast 25 to 35 minutes or until chicken is done (at least 175°F in thigh). Remove from oven. Roast vegetables 10 to 15 minutes more or until tender and golden.

6. Cover chicken with foil and let stand 15 minutes. If desired, remove zest from remaining lemon. To serve, remove and discard skin from chicken. Carve chicken and drizzle with reserved lemon juice and pan juices. Serve with vegetables and top with lemon zest and additional fresh thyme and rosemary.

PER SERVING *(3 oz. chicken + 1 cup vegetables each)* **CAL** 296, **FAT** 7 g (2 g sat. fat), **CHOL** 96 mg, **SODIUM** 333 mg, **CARB** 26 g (4 g fiber, 5 g sugars), **PRO** 32 g

STEP 1
Tighten skin
With the chicken on its back, slide twine underneath its middle. Pull ends of the twine over the wings and cross the string around the top of the breast, tightening the skin.

STEP 2
Secure wings
Bring ends of twine above wings, running them along sides of the breast. Cross ends of the twine, pulling tightly up and under the tip of the breast.

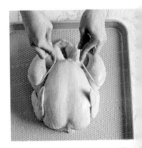

STEP 3
Loop the legs
Bring the ends of the string under the legs, then loop over the tops of the legs. Cross and tighten. The thighs will pop out.

STEP 4
Flip and finish
Flip the bird over and tie the strings in a knot around the tail. Snip off the ends. Cook the chicken breast side up.

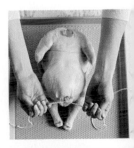

Creamy Polenta with Chicken-Porcini Sauce

25 g
CARB

SERVES 4
HANDS ON 55 min.
TOTAL 55 min.

½ cup reduced-sodium chicken broth
⅓ cup dried porcini mushrooms
¼ tsp. garlic powder
⅛ tsp. salt
⅛ tsp. black pepper
1 lb. chicken breast tenderloins
1 Tbsp. canola oil
4 cups thinly sliced fresh cremini mushrooms
1 medium shallot, thinly sliced
¼ cup dry white wine or reduced-sodium chicken broth
½ cup half-and-half

1 recipe Creamy Polenta
1 oz. Parmesan cheese, shaved
Fresh Italian parsley and/or snipped fresh rosemary

1. In a bowl microwave broth just until boiling. Add dried mushrooms; cover and let stand 10 minutes. Drain porcini mushrooms through a paper towel-lined sieve, reserving broth. Rinse porcini mushrooms. Chop mushrooms; set aside.

2. Meanwhile in a bowl combine garlic powder, salt, and pepper. Sprinkle over chicken. In a 10-inch skillet heat oil over medium-high. Add chicken. Cook 8 to 10 minutes or until chicken is done (165°), turning once. Transfer chicken to a plate; cover to keep warm.

3. Add fresh mushrooms and shallot to skillet. Cook over medium-high 5 to 7 minutes or until mushrooms are tender and starting to brown, stirring occasionally. Carefully add wine. Cook 3 to 4 minutes or until wine is nearly evaporated. Add chopped mushrooms, ¼ cup of the reserved mushroom broth, and the half-and-half. Bring to boiling. Boil gently, uncovered, about 5 minutes or until slightly thickened, stirring frequently.

4. Serve chicken and porcini sauce with Creamy Polenta. Top with shaved Parmesan cheese and Italian parsley and/or rosemary.

Creamy Polenta In a medium saucepan bring 3 cups water and ¼ tsp. salt to boiling. Slowly add ¾ cup coarse-ground yellow cornmeal to boiling water, whisking constantly. Cook and stir until mixture returns to boiling. Reduce heat to medium-low. Cook about 25 minutes or until mixture is very thick and tender, stirring frequently and adjusting heat as needed to maintain a slow boil. Add additional water as needed to maintain a soft, creamy texture. Stir in ⅓ cup finely shredded Parmesan cheese.

PER SERVING (¾ cup polenta + 3 oz. cooked chicken + ½ cup sauce each) **CAL** 394, **FAT** 15 g (5 g sat. fat), **CHOL** 104 mg, **SODIUM** 619 mg, **CARB** 25 g (5 g fiber, 4 g sugars), **PRO** 38 g

Creamy Polenta with Chicken-Porcini Sauce

Kale, Grapefruit, and Chicken Salad

Kale, Grapefruit, and Chicken Salad

25 g
CARB

SERVES	4
HANDS ON	30 min.
TOTAL	35 min.

- 2 red grapefruit or blood oranges
- 2 8-oz. skinless, boneless chicken breast halves, halved horizontally
- 2 Tbsp. olive oil
- 4 tsp. honey
- ½ tsp. black pepper
- 6 cups torn fresh kale
- ½ tsp. salt
  Nonstick cooking spray
- ½ cup pomegranate seeds
- ½ cup halved and very thinly sliced red onion

1. Remove zest from grapefruit. Peel and section grapefruit.
2. Place chicken in a resealable plastic bag set in a shallow dish. For marinade, combine 4 tsp. of the grapefruit zest, 4 tsp. of the grapefruit juice, and 2 tsp. of the oil. Pour marinade over chicken. Seal bag; turn to coat chicken. Marinate in the refrigerator until needed.
3. For dressing, whisk together honey, pepper, and the remaining grapefruit juice.
4. In a large bowl combine kale, salt, and the remaining 4 tsp. oil. Using your hands, massage oil mixture into kale 1 to 2 minutes or until kale begins to soften.
5. Drain chicken, discarding marinade. Coat a 12-inch nonstick skillet or grill pan with cooking spray; heat over medium-high. Add chicken; cook 6 to 8 minutes or until done (165°F), turning once. Remove from heat and let stand 5 minutes. Thinly slice chicken.
6. To serve, add grapefruit sections, chicken, dressing, pomegranate seeds, and onion to kale; toss gently to combine.

Tip To section grapefruit, cut the peel away with a sharp knife. Over a bowl to catch juice, cut between sections and membranes to release sections. Squeeze membranes to get any remaining juice.

PER SERVING (*2 cups each*) **CAL** 312, **FAT** 11 g (2 g sat. fat), **CHOL** 83 mg, **SODIUM** 382 mg, **CARB** 25 g (4 g fiber, 14 g sugars), **PRO** 31 g

Cran-Chipotle Turkey Sandwich

32 g
CARB

SERVES 2
TOTAL 15 min.

- 1 cup shredded or chopped leftover roast turkey breast (5 oz.)
- 3 Tbsp. canned whole berry cranberry sauce
- ½ to 1 tsp. canned chipotle pepper in adobo sauce, finely chopped
- 2 multigrain thin sandwich rolls, toasted
- 2 leaf lettuce leaves

1. In a small saucepan combine turkey, cranberry sauce, and chipotle pepper. Cook, covered, over medium 5 minutes or until heated, stirring occasionally.
2. To serve, fill sandwich rolls with lettuce and turkey mixture.

PER SERVING (1 sandwich each) **CAL** 242, **FAT** 2 g (0 g sat. fat), **CHOL** 50 mg, **SODIUM** 327 mg, **CARB** 32 g (5 g fiber, 10 g sugars), **PRO** 26 g

Turkey Green Bean Shepherd's Pie

31 g
CARB

SERVES 4
HANDS ON 10 min.
TOTAL 45 min.

- 12 oz. shredded leftover roast turkey breast (about 1 cup)
- 2 cups leftover cooked green beans
- 2 cups leftover mashed potatoes
- ½ cup shredded reduced-fat cheddar cheese
  Snipped fresh chives (optional)

1. Preheat oven to 375°F. In four 12- to 14-oz. ramekins or individual gratin dishes layer the turkey and green beans. Top with mashed potatoes, spreading evenly. Cover with foil. Bake 30 minutes. Remove foil and sprinkle with cheese. Bake, uncovered, about 5 minutes more or until cheese is melted. If desired, sprinkle with chives.

PER SERVING (2 cups each) **CAL** 344, **FAT** 11 g (6 g sat. fat), **CHOL** 85 mg, **SODIUM** 422 mg, **CARB** 31 g (4 g fiber, 4 g sugars), **PRO** 34 g

Turkey-Broccoli Salad with Grapes

20 g
CARB

SERVES 6
TOTAL 20 min.

- 1 12-oz. pkg. shredded broccoli slaw mix
- 1 lb. shredded cooked turkey breast
- 1½ cups seedless red grapes, halved
- 1 cup coarsely shredded carrots
- ½ cup light poppy seed salad dressing
- 1 Tbsp. cider vinegar
- ¼ cup sliced or slivered almonds, toasted, or sunflower kernels
- ⅛ tsp. coarsely ground black pepper

1. In an extra-large bowl combine broccoli slaw, turkey, grapes, and carrots. Drizzle with dressing and vinegar; toss to coat.
2. Serve immediately or cover and chill up to 24 hours. Sprinkle with almonds and pepper before serving.

Tip To toast nuts, preheat oven to 350°F. Spread nuts in a shallow baking pan lined with parchment paper. Bake 5 to 10 minutes or until golden, shaking pan once or twice.

PER SERVING (1⅔ cups each) **CAL** 223, **FAT** 6 g (1 g sat. fat), **CHOL** 56 mg, **SODIUM** 258 mg, **CARB** 20 g (3 g fiber, 14 g sugars), **PRO** 25 g

Roasted Turkey and Brussels Sprouts Sheet-Pan Dinner
recipe, *p. 78*

Roasted Turkey and Brussels Sprouts Sheet-Pan Dinner

31 g CARB

SERVES 6
HANDS ON 15 min.
TOTAL 50 min.

Nonstick cooking spray
½ tsp. onion powder
½ tsp. garlic powder
½ tsp. black pepper
½ tsp. salt
1½ lb. turkey tenderloins
3 carrots, peeled and cut into bite-size pieces
2 tsp. olive oil
½ cup orange marmalade
1 Tbsp. grated fresh ginger
1 lb. fresh Brussels sprouts, trimmed and halved
Orange wedges

1. Preheat oven to 400°F. Lightly coat a 13×9-inch baking pan with cooking spray. In a bowl stir together onion powder, garlic powder, pepper, and ¼ tsp. of the salt. Sprinkle evenly over turkey; rub in with your fingers. Place turkey on one side of the prepared pan.
2. In a bowl toss carrots with olive oil to coat. Place carrots next to turkey in baking pan. Roast, uncovered, 15 minutes.
3. Meanwhile, in a medium saucepan combine orange marmalade, ginger, and the remaining ¼ tsp. salt. Cook and stir over low until melted. Reserve 2 Tbsp. of the marmalade mixture. Add Brussels sprouts to the saucepan; stir to coat. Add Brussels sprouts to carrots in baking pan after 15 minutes of roasting; stir to combine. Brush turkey with reserved marmalade mixture.
4. Roast, uncovered, 20 to 25 minutes more or until turkey is done (165°F) and vegetables are tender, stirring vegetables once. Slice tenderloins and serve with vegetables and orange wedges.

PER SERVING (3 oz. cooked turkey + about ¾ cup vegetables each) **CAL** 260, **FAT** 3 g (1 g sat. fat), **CHOL** 51 mg, **SODIUM** 325 mg, **CARB** 31 g (5 g fiber, 21 g sugars), **PRO** 30 g

Dijon Turkey with Apple-Sage Wheat Berries

51 g CARB

SERVES 6
HANDS ON 25 min.
SLOW COOK 8 hr.

3 cups unsalted chicken stock
1½ cups wheat berries
1½ cups water
¾ tsp. salt
¼ tsp. black pepper
1 cup chopped onion
1 cup sliced celery
1 cup chopped carrots
1¼ to 1½ lb. turkey breast tenderloin
2 Tbsp. apple jelly
2 Tbsp. Dijon-style mustard
2 Tbsp. olive oil
1 Tbsp. snipped fresh sage
1 Tbsp. red wine vinegar
1 clove garlic, minced
2 medium firm red cooking apples, cut into ½-inch wedges
6 Tbsp. chopped toasted walnuts (optional)

1. In a 5- to 6-qt. slow cooker combine stock, wheat berries, the water, ½ tsp. of the salt, and the pepper. Add onion, celery, and carrots. Cover and cook on low 6 to 8 hours.
2. Meanwhile, place turkey in a resealable plastic bag set in a shallow dish. For marinade, in a small bowl whisk together jelly, mustard, 1 Tbsp. of the oil, the sage, vinegar, garlic, and the remaining ¼ tsp. salt. Pour marinade over turkey. Seal bag; turn to coat turkey. Marinate in refrigerator 6 to 8 hours.
3. Drain turkey, reserving marinade. In a 10-inch skillet heat the remaining 1 Tbsp. oil over medium-high. Add turkey; cook about 6 minutes or until browned, turning once.
4. Drain wheat berry mixture; reserve cooking liquid. Return wheat berry mixture and ½ cup of the cooking liquid to cooker. Add turkey, the reserved marinade, and apples. Turn cooker to high. Cover and cook about 2 hours or until turkey is done (165°F).
5. Remove and thinly slice turkey. Using a slotted spoon, transfer apple

mixture to plates; add turkey. Drizzle with the remaining cooking liquid and, if desired, sprinkle with walnuts and additional sage.

Dijon Turkey with
Apple-Sage Wheat Berries

Tip To use the cooker's high-heat setting, prepare wheat berry mixture as directed in Step 1, except cover and cook on high 4 hours. Continue as directed, except marinate turkey in refrigerator 4 hours before browning. In Step 4, cover and cook mixture in cooker on high about 1¼ hours or until turkey is done (165°F). Serve as directed.

PER SERVING *(3 oz. turkey + 1 cup apple mixture each)* **CAL** 381, **FAT** 7 g (1 g sat. fat), **CHOL** 50 mg, **SODIUM** 574 mg, **CARB** 51 g (9 g fiber, 13 g sugars), **PRO** 31 g

Turkey and Vegetable Meat Loaf

9g CARB | **SERVES** 6
HANDS ON 20 min.
TOTAL 55 min.

- 1 8-oz. can tomato sauce
- ½ cup reduced-sodium chicken stock or broth
- 1 Tbsp. packed light brown sugar*
- 1 Tbsp. cider vinegar
- ½ tsp. dried Italian seasoning, crushed
- ½ cup finely chopped yellow onion
- ½ cup finely chopped zucchini
- ¼ cup seasoned fine dry bread crumbs
- ¼ cup finely chopped red sweet pepper
- 1 Tbsp. minced garlic
- 1 tsp. dried thyme, crushed
- ½ tsp. salt
- ½ tsp. black pepper
- ⅛ tsp. ground allspice
- 2 lb. 93% lean ground turkey

1. For sauce, in the cooking pot of a 6-qt. electric pressure cooker combine the first five ingredients (through Italian seasoning).

2. In a large bowl combine the next nine ingredients (through allspice). Add ground turkey; mix well. Shape mixture into a round loaf and place in cooker.

3. Cover with lid and lock securely. Select high pressure and set timer for 25 minutes (timer will start after cooker has come up to pressure). Allow pressure to release naturally for 10 minutes before quick-releasing the remaining pressure. Unlock and remove lid. Serve meat loaf with sauce.

Note We do not recommend using a stove-top pressure cooker for this recipe.

Turkey and Vegetable Meat Loaf

Oven Directions To bake meat loaf, preheat oven to 350°F. Line a 13×9-inch baking pan with foil. Prepare as directed, except omit the chicken stock and combine the sauce mixture in Step 1 in a bowl. In the prepared pan lightly pat turkey mixture in Step 2 into a 9×5-inch loaf. Bake 45 minutes. Spoon sauce mixture over meat loaf. Bake 15 to 25 minutes more or until a thermometer inserted in center of loaf registers 165°F. Let meat loaf stand 10 minutes before serving.

PER SERVING (5 oz. meat loaf + ⅓ cup sauce each) **CAL** 277, **FAT** 13 g (3 g sat. fat), **CHOL** 112 mg, **SODIUM** 605 mg, **CARB** 10 g (1 g fiber, 5 g sugars), **PRO** 30 g

*****Sugar Sub** Choose Splenda Brown Sugar Blend. Follow package directions to use 1 Tbsp. equivalent.

PER SERVING WITH SUB Same as above, except **CAL** 273, **CARB** 9 g (4 g sugars), **SODIUM** 604 mg

Rosemary, Cherry, and Ham Stuffing Cups

30 g CARB

SERVES 6
HANDS ON 40 min.
TOTAL 1 hr. 5 min.

- 1 Tbsp. butter
- 2 cups ½-inch cubes butternut squash (about 9 oz.)
- ½ cup chopped onion
- ¼ cup chopped celery
- ¼ cup slivered almonds
- ¾ cup ¼-inch cubes cooked ham
- ¼ cup snipped dried cherries
- 1 tsp. snipped fresh rosemary or ¼ tsp. dried rosemary, crushed
- ¼ tsp. salt
- ¼ tsp. cracked black pepper
- 5 cups ½-inch cubes country-style whole wheat bread, dried
- 1 egg, lightly beaten
- ¾ cup reduced-sodium chicken broth

1. Preheat oven to 350°F. Line twelve 2½-inch muffin cups with foil bake cups. In a 10-inch skillet melt butter over medium. Add squash, onion, and celery; cook 6 minutes, stirring occasionally. Stir in almonds; cook 3 minutes more. Stir in the next five ingredients (through pepper).
2. In a bowl combine squash mixture and bread cubes. Add egg and broth, tossing gently to moisten. Spoon about ⅓ cup of the mixture into each prepared muffin cup; press lightly.
3. Bake about 20 minutes or until heated (165°F). Cool in cups on a wire rack 5 minutes. Serve warm.

Tip For dried bread, spread cubes in a 15×10-inch baking pan. Cover lightly; let stand overnight. Bake in a 300°F oven 10 to 15 minutes or until dried, stirring twice; cool. Bread will continue to dry and crisp as it cools.

To Make Ahead Prepare cups through Step 3. Cover with foil and chill up to 24 hours. Bake as directed.

PER SERVING *(2 stuffing cups each)*
CAL 233, **FAT** 8 g (3 g sat. fat), **CHOL** 47 mg, **SODIUM** 588 mg, **CARB** 30 g (5 g fiber, 8 g sugars), **PRO** 11 g

Rosemary, Cherry, and Ham Stuffing Cups

Pork Tenderloin with Apple-Thyme Sweet Potatoes

44 g CARB

SERVES 4
HANDS ON 35 min.
TOTAL 1 hr.

1 1-lb. pork tenderloin, trimmed
½ tsp. kosher salt
¼ tsp. black pepper
1 Tbsp. canola oil
1 lb. sweet potatoes, peeled and cut into ½-inch pieces
2 cups chopped sweet onions
2 cloves garlic, minced
¼ cup apple cider
¼ cup cider vinegar
2 medium apples, such as Granny Smith or Honeycrisp, cored and cut into eighths
2 sprigs fresh thyme
2 bay leaves

1. Preheat oven to 350°F. Sprinkle meat with salt and pepper. In a 12-inch oven-going skillet heat oil over medium-high. Add tenderloin; cook 5 minutes or until browned on all sides. Transfer to a plate.

2. Add sweet potatoes to skillet. Cook over medium 2 minutes, stirring occasionally. Add onions and garlic; cook 3 to 5 minutes or until onions are tender, stirring occasionally. Stir in cider and vinegar. Return meat and any juices to skillet. Add the remaining ingredients.

3. Transfer skillet to oven. Bake 20 to 25 minutes or until pork is done (145°F), turning and basting tenderloin occasionally. Remove and discard thyme and bay leaves.

4. Transfer tenderloin to a cutting board. Cover with foil and let stand 3 minutes. Slice meat. Serve with potato mixture and, if desired, top with additional thyme.

PER SERVING *(3½ oz. cooked meat + 1¼ cups potato mixture each)* **CAL** 342, **FAT** 6 g (1 g sat. fat), **CHOL** 73 mg, **SODIUM** 257 mg, **CARB** 44 g (7 g fiber, 18 g sugars), **PRO** 27 g

QUICK TIP Think pink for the doneness of pork tenderloin and loin. These lean cuts stay deliciously juicy when cooked to an internal temperature of 145°F. Letting them stand covered with foil for a few minutes after roasting allows their juices to settle back into the center of the meat.

Pork and Squash Salad

Bacon-Wrapped Pork Tenderloin

28 g CARB

SERVES 4
HANDS ON 20 min.
TOTAL 45 min.

- ¼ cup cherry preserves, large pieces snipped
- 1 tsp. red wine vinegar
- 10 slices lower-sodium, less-fat bacon
- 1 1-lb. pork tenderloin, trimmed
- 1 Tbsp. olive oil
- 8 oz. green beans, trimmed if desired
- ¼ cup reduced-sodium chicken broth
- 2 Tbsp. honey
- ¼ tsp. salt
- ¼ cup sliced almonds, toasted

1. Preheat oven to 425°F. Line a shallow roasting pan with foil. Place a rack in lined pan. In a bowl stir together cherry preserves and vinegar.
2. Lay bacon side by side on a work surface, overlapping slightly. Place tenderloin crosswise on bacon and roll up, wrapping bacon around tenderloin. Place tenderloin, bacon ends down, on rack in the prepared pan. Roast 20 minutes. Brush top of wrapped tenderloin with preserves mixture. Roast 5 to 10 minutes more or until bacon is crisp and pork is done (145°F). Remove from oven; let stand 3 minutes.
3. Meanwhile, in a 10-inch skillet heat oil over medium-high. Add green beans; cook and stir 3 to 5 minutes or just until crisp-tender. Add broth, honey, and salt. Cook and stir about 3 minutes more or until liquid is nearly evaporated. Stir in almonds. Serve green beans with sliced tenderloin.

PER SERVING (3 oz. cooked meat + about ½ cup green beans each) **CAL** 351, **FAT** 12 g (3 g sat. fat), **CHOL** 82 mg, **SODIUM** 426 mg, **CARB** 28 g (2 g fiber, 20 g sugars), **PRO** 31 g

Pork and Squash Salad

31 g CARB

SERVES 4
HANDS ON 25 min.
TOTAL 50 min.

- 2 Tbsp. balsamic vinegar
- 4 tsp. olive oil
- ½ tsp. salt
- ½ tsp. ground cinnamon
- ½ tsp. black pepper
- 1½ cups ¾-inch pieces butternut squash
- ½ cup chopped onion
- 2 8-oz. boneless pork loin chop, cut 1 inch thick and trimmed
- 2 Tbsp. pure maple syrup
- 2 Tbsp. chopped pecans (optional)
- 6 cups mixed baby salad greens
- ½ cup dried cranberries

1. Place a 12-inch cast-iron skillet in the oven. Preheat oven to 425°F.
2. Meanwhile, whisk together the first five ingredients (through pepper). In a small bowl toss squash and onion with 4 tsp. of the vinegar mixture. Carefully arrange squash mixture around edges of hot skillet. Roast 5 minutes.
3. Brush both sides of chops with 2 teaspoon of the vinegar mixture. Place chops in center of hot skillet. Roast 18 to 20 minutes more or until squash is tender and browned, turning chops and stirring vegetables once.
4. Drizzle maple syrup over chops and vegetables. If using, sprinkle pecans over vegetables. Roast 1 to 2 minutes more or until a thermometer inserted in chops registers 145°F and pecans are toasted. Remove from oven and let stand 3 minutes. Thinly slice chops.
5. In a medium bowl toss together salad greens, cranberries, meat, vegetables, and the remaining vinegar mixture.

PER SERVING (2 cups each) **CAL** 306, **FAT** 9 g (2 g sat. fat), **CHOL** 75 mg, **SODIUM** 363 mg, **CARB** 31 g (4 g fiber, 19 g sugars), **PRO** 27 g

**Bacon-Wrapped
Pork Tenderloin**

QUICK TIP If the sweet potato is long and slender instead of short and fat, cut it in half lengthwise instead of in quarters before slicing.

Grilled Pork Chops with Warm Sweet Potato-Kale Salad

Grilled Pork Chops with Warm Sweet Potato-Kale Salad

35 g CARB

SERVES 4
HANDS ON 1 hr.
TOTAL 1 hr.

- 1 medium (10 to 12 oz.) sweet potato, peeled
- 4 strips reduced-fat, reduced-sodium bacon, coarsely chopped
- ¼ cup thinly sliced shallots
- 4 cups coarsely chopped, stemmed kale
- 1 medium red cooking apple, cored and coarsely chopped
- 2 Tbsp. cider vinegar
- 2 tsp. spicy brown mustard
- 1 recipe Maple-Ginger Cherry Sauce
  Fresh thyme (optional)
- 4 ¾- to 1-inch-thick bone-in pork chops (2 lb. total)
- 2 tsp. snipped fresh thyme
- ¼ tsp. salt
- ¼ tsp. black pepper

1. Cut sweet potato lengthwise into quarters. Cut each quarter crosswise into ¼-inch-thick slices.

2. In a 12-inch nonstick skillet cook bacon over medium until crisp. Drain bacon on paper towels. Remove and discard all but 2 Tbsp. drippings in the skillet. Add sweet potato slices; cook about 5 minutes or until potatoes are lightly golden, stirring occasionally. Add shallots and apples; cook 3 minutes. Stir in kale; cook 2 to 3 minutes or until potatoes and apples are tender, stirring occasionally.

3. In a bowl whisk together vinegar and mustard. Drizzle over sweet potato mixture; toss to combine. Remove from heat. Stir in reserved bacon. Keep warm.

4. Trim fat from pork chops. In a bowl combine 1 tsp. of the thyme, the salt, and pepper. Sprinkle over both sides of chops, rubbing in with your fingers.

5. Grill pork chops, covered, over medium 8 to 10 minutes or until done (145°F), turning once. Cover chops with foil; let stand 3 minutes.

6. Serve pork chops with sweet potato salad and Maple-Ginger Cherry Sauce. Top with remaining 1 tsp. thyme.

Maple-Ginger Cherry Sauce In a small saucepan combine ¾ cup frozen unsweetened pitted tart red cherries and 2 Tbsp. water; bring to boiling; reduce heat. Simmer, covered, about 5 minutes or until cherries start to break down. If needed, mash lightly with a fork. In a bowl stir together 1 Tbsp. water and 1 tsp cornstarch; add 2 Tbsp. reduced-calorie maple-flavor pancake syrup and 2 tsp. finely chopped fresh ginger. Stir into cherry mixture; cook and stir 5 to 6 minutes more or until sauce is slightly thickened and bubbly. Remove from heat. Cool about 5 minutes before serving.

PER SERVING (1 pork chop +1 cup salad + 4 tsp. cherry sauce each) CAL 419, FAT 15 g (5 g sat. fat), CHOL 85 mg, SODIUM 421 mg, CARB 35 g (7 g fiber, 16 g sugars), PRO 36 g

Pork Roast and Harvest Vegetables

23 g
CARB

SERVES 6
HANDS ON 30 min.
SLOW COOK 10 hr.

- 1 3- to 3½-lb. boneless pork shoulder roast, trimmed
- ½ tsp. salt
- ¼ tsp. black pepper
- 1 Tbsp. vegetable oil
- 3 medium parsnips, peeled and cut into ½-inch pieces
- 3 medium carrots, cut into ½-inch pieces
- 2 stalks celery, cut into ½-inch pieces
- 1 large green sweet pepper, cut into bite-size pieces
- 3 Tbsp. quick-cooking tapioca, crushed
- ¾ cup 50%-less-sodium beef broth
- ½ of a 6-oz. can (⅓ cup) frozen apple juice concentrate, thawed
- ¼ tsp. ground cinnamon
- 1 recipe Quick Orange Gremolata (optional)

1. If necessary, cut meat to fit into a 5- to 6-qt. slow cooker. Sprinkle meat with ¼ tsp. each of the salt and black pepper. In a 12-inch skillet heat oil over medium-high. Add meat; cook until browned on all sides. Drain off fat.

2. In slow cooker combine the next four ingredients (through sweet pepper); sprinkle with tapioca. In a small bowl combine the next three ingredients (through cinnamon) and the remaining ¼ tsp. each salt and black pepper; pour over vegetables. Add meat.

3. Cover and cook on low 10 to 12 hours or high 5 to 6 hours.

4. Using a slotted spoon, transfer meat and vegetables to a serving platter. Strain cooking liquid; skim off fat. Drizzle some of the cooking liquid over meat. Pass the remaining cooking liquid. If desired, top with Quick Orange Gremolata.

PER SERVING (6 oz. cooked meat + ½ cup vegetables + ¼ cup cooking liquid each) CAL 401, FAT 12 g (4 g sat. fat), CHOL 145 mg, SODIUM 445 mg, CARB 23 g (4 g fiber, 10 g sugars), PRO 48 g

Quick Orange Gremolata In a bowl combine 1 Tbsp. snipped fresh parsley, 1 tsp. orange zest, and ½ tsp. minced garlic.

Lemon-Herb Roasted Salmon

13 g
CARB

SERVES 4	
HANDS ON 20 min.	
TOTAL 35 min.	

- 1 1-lb. fresh or frozen skinless salmon fillet
- 2 Tbsp. olive oil
- 1½ tsp. dried oregano, crushed
- ¼ tsp. salt
- ⅛ tsp. black pepper
- 2 cups grape or cherry tomatoes, halved
- 2 cups broccoli florets
- 2 cloves garlic, minced
- 1 lemon
- 2 Tbsp. snipped fresh basil
- 1 Tbsp. snipped fresh parsley
- 1 Tbsp. honey

1. Thaw salmon, if frozen. Preheat oven to 400°F. Line a 15×10-inch baking pan with parchment paper. Rinse salmon; pat dry with paper towels. Place salmon in prepared pan. Drizzle with 1 Tbsp. of the oil and sprinkle with ¾ tsp. of the oregano, the salt, and pepper.
2. In a bowl combine tomatoes, broccoli, garlic, and the remaining 1 Tbsp. oil and ¾ tsp. oregano; toss to coat. Place in pan with salmon. Roast salmon and vegetables, uncovered, 15 to 18 minutes or just until salmon flakes.
3. Meanwhile, remove 1 tsp. zest and squeeze 3 Tbsp. juice from lemon. In a small bowl combine lemon zest and juice and the remaining ingredients. Spoon over salmon and vegetables.

PER SERVING (3½ oz. salmon + ½ cup vegetables each) **CAL** 276, **FAT** 14 g (2 g sat. fat), **CHOL** 62 mg, **SODIUM** 362 mg, **CARB** 13 g (3 g fiber, 8 g sugars), **PRO** 25 g

« **QUICK TIP** You can cut the salmon fillet into individual pieces before roasting. To serve, slide a spatula between the skin and fish and leave the skin in the pan.

Roasted Salmon with White Bean Ragout

18 g
CARB

SERVES 8
HANDS ON 30 min.
TOTAL 34 min.

- 2 Tbsp. olive oil
- ¾ cup chopped onion
- ¾ cup chopped red sweet pepper
- 3 Tbsp. tomato paste
- 1 tsp. salt
- ¾ tsp. black pepper
- 2 cups coarsely chopped Swiss chard
- 2 15-oz. cans no-salt-added cannellini beans (white kidney beans), rinsed and drained
- ½ cup reduced-sodium chicken broth or vegetable broth Nonstick cooking spray
- 8 4-oz. fresh or frozen skinless salmon fillets, thawed
- 2 cups halved cherry tomatoes
- 8 tsp. grated Pecorino Romano cheese

1. In a 12-inch nonstick skillet heat 1 Tbsp. of the oil over medium. Add onion and sweet pepper; cook about 5 minutes or until tender, stirring occasionally. Stir in tomato paste, ½ tsp. of the salt, and ¼ tsp. of the black pepper; cook and stir 2 minutes. Stir in Swiss chard. Cook and stir about 1 minute or until chard is wilted. Stir in beans and broth; cool. Cover and chill up to 3 days.

2. To serve, preheat broiler. Line a baking sheet with foil; coat foil with cooking spray.

3. Rinse fish; pat dry. Measure thickness of fish. Place on the prepared baking sheet. Brush with the remaining 1 Tbsp. oil and sprinkle with the remaining ½ tsp. each salt and black pepper. Broil 4 inches from heat 4 to 6 minutes per ½-inch thickness or until fish flakes easily (if fish is 1 inch or more thick, turn once).

4. Meanwhile, in a 10-inch nonstick skillet cook bean mixture over medium 5 minutes or until heated, stirring occasionally. If needed, thin with up to ½ cup water to desired consistency. Stir in tomatoes.

5. Arrange fish on bean mixture. Sprinkle with cheese and additional black pepper.

PER SERVING *(1 salmon fillet + ⅔ cup bean mixture each)* **CAL** 299, **FAT** 12 g (2 g sat. fat), **CHOL** 64 mg, **SODIUM** 501 mg, **CARB** 18 g (5 g fiber, 3 g sugars), **PRO** 29 g

Roasted Salmon with White Bean Ragout

Gingered Vegetable Curry

35 g
CARB

SERVES 4
TOTAL 35 min.

- 2 tsp. canola oil
- ½ cup chopped onion
- ½ cup ½-inch slices carrot
- 4 tsp. red curry paste
- 4 tsp. grated fresh ginger
- ½ tsp. salt

Gingered Vegetable Curry

2 cups unsweetened light coconut milk
1 cup small cauliflower florets
1 cup 2-inch pieces green beans
1 cup canned garbanzo beans (chickpeas), rinsed and drained
4 tsp. lime juice
1⅓ cups hot cooked brown rice
¼ cup fresh cilantro leaves
4 tsp. coarsely chopped peanuts (optional)

1. In a 12-inch skillet heat oil over medium. Add onion and carrot; cook 5 to 7 minutes or until onion is tender, stirring occasionally. Stir in the next three ingredients (through salt): cook and stir 1 minute more.

2. Add coconut milk; bring to boiling. Add cauliflower, green beans, and garbanzo beans; reduce heat. Simmer, uncovered, about 8 minutes or just until vegetables are tender and milk is slightly thickened. Stir in lime juice.

3. Serve vegetable mixture over rice and sprinkle with cilantro and, if desired, peanuts.

PER SERVING (¾ cup vegetable mixture + ⅓ cup rice each) **CAL** 259, **FAT** 11 g (6 g sat. fat), **CHOL** 0 mg, **SODIUM** 535 mg, **CARB** 35 g (6 g fiber, 7 g sugars), **PRO** 8 g

Roasted Mushroom, Spinach, and Ricotta Tart

28 g
CARB

SERVES 6
HANDS ON 30 min.
TOTAL 1 hr. 45 min.

Nonstick cooking spray
1¼ cups unbleached all-purpose flour
2 Tbsp. dry-roasted sunflower kernels
2 tsp. snipped fresh thyme
¼ tsp. baking powder
½ tsp. salt
¼ cup olive oil
¼ cup cold water
⅔ cup fat-free ricotta cheese
1 egg
2 egg whites
¼ cup fresh basil leaves
3 Tbsp. grated Parmesan cheese
¼ tsp. black pepper
3 8-oz. pkg. assorted fresh mushrooms, thinly sliced
1 Tbsp. olive oil
¼ tsp. salt
1 6-oz. pkg. fresh spinach
¼ cup dry Marsala

1. Preheat oven to 450°F. Coat a 9-inch pie plate with cooking spray.
2. For pastry, in a food processor combine the next four ingredients (through baking powder) and ¼ tsp. of the salt. Cover and pulse until sunflower kernels are chopped. In a glass measuring cup combine the ¼ cup oil and the water. With processor running, slowly add oil mixture through feed tube, processing just until mixture comes together (do not overprocess).
3. Press pastry onto bottom and sides of the prepared pie plate. Prick bottom a few times with a fork. Bake 10 minutes. Cool on a wire rack.
4. Meanwhile, for filling, in food processor process ricotta cheese, egg, egg whites, basil, 2 Tbsp. of the Parmesan cheese, and the pepper until smooth.

5. Place mushrooms in a large roasting pan. Drizzle with the 1 Tbsp. oil and sprinkle with the remaining ¼ tsp. salt. Roast about 25 minutes or until mushroom liquid is nearly evaporated, stirring twice. Stir in spinach and Marsala. Roast about 10 minutes more or until Marsala is nearly evaporated, stirring once. Remove from oven. Reduce oven temperature to 375°F.
6. Spread filling in baked pastry shell. Top with mushroom mixture and the remaining 1 Tbsp. Parmesan cheese. Bake 25 to 30 minutes or just until filling is set. Let stand 15 minutes before serving.

PER SERVING (1 wedge each) **CAL** 300, **FAT** 15 g (2 g sat. fat), **CHOL** 40 mg, **SODIUM** 402 mg, **CARB** 28 g (3 g fiber, 4 g sugars), **PRO** 13 g

Brussels Sprouts and
Goat Cheese Flatbread

Brussels Sprouts and Goat Cheese Flatbread

23 g
CARB

SERVES	2
HANDS ON	10 min.
TOTAL	16 min.

1 artisan thin pizza crust,
 such as Flatout
1 oz. soft goat cheese (chèvre)
½ cup thinly sliced Brussels
 sprouts
3 Tbsp. snipped dried apricots
2 Tbsp. chopped walnuts,
 toasted
½ tsp. honey
½ tsp. lime zest

1. Preheat oven to 425°F. Bake crust
on oven rack 4 to 6 minutes or until
golden and crisp. Spread with cheese
and top with the remaining
ingredients.

Tip Double or triple the recipe to serve
four or six. Or cut the flatbread into
smaller portions to serve as an
appetizer.

PER SERVING (½ of a flatbread each)
CAL 190, **FAT** 8 g (3 g sat. fat), **CHOL** 7 mg,
SODIUM 266 mg, **CARB** 23 g (3 g fiber,
10 g sugars), **PRO** 7 g

5

SEASONAL
SIDES & SALADS

Bring more to your holiday table than basic steamed veggies and
green salads. Using a simple sauce or a crunchy topping takes
humble vegetables to new heights. Seasonal ingredients like
cranberries, citrus, pomegranate seeds, Brussels sprouts, and more
add festive flavor and light up everyone's taste buds.

QUICK TIP If using morel mushrooms, place mushrooms in a pan or bowl. Cover with water and add a dash salt. Soak mushrooms 10 to 15 minutes. Drain, rinse, and repeat two more times. Pat mushrooms dry. If necessary, trim ends of stems.

Flash-Braised Vegetable Medley

Flash-Braised Vegetable Medley

19 g CARB | **SERVES** 6
TOTAL 25 min.

- 2 Tbsp. butter
- 1½ lb. young spring carrots, trimmed and scrubbed, or large carrots, peeled and cut into 3-inch pieces
- 8 oz. button mushrooms, quartered or halved if large, and/or other mushrooms, such as oyster and/or morel
- 6 oz. pearl or whole boiling onions, peeled
- 3 cloves garlic, chopped
- ½ cup dry white wine or chicken broth
- 1 cup unsalted chicken broth
- 2 Tbsp. snipped fresh marjoram
- ¼ tsp. kosher salt
- ¼ tsp. black pepper
- 8 oz. fresh asparagus, trimmed and cut into 2- to 3-inch pieces
  Lemon wedges

1. In a 12-inch skillet melt butter over medium. Add carrots and mushrooms; cook 3 minutes, stirring occasionally. Add onions and garlic; cook and stir 2 minutes. Increase heat to medium-high. Carefully add wine; cook 1 minute or until wine has almost evaporated. Add chicken broth, 1 Tbsp. of the marjoram, the salt, and pepper; reduce heat to medium. Cover and cook 8 to 10 minutes or until vegetables are fork-tender.
2. Remove from heat. Add asparagus; cover. Let stand 5 minutes. Sprinkle with the remaining 1 Tbsp. marjoram. Serve with lemon wedges.

PER SERVING (1½ cups each) **CAL** 136, **FAT** 4 g (3 g sat. fat), **CHOL** 10 mg, **SODIUM** 173 mg, **CARB** 19 g (4 g fiber, 8 g sugars), **PRO** 4 g

Lemon Toasted Farro and Cauliflower Pilaf

23 g CARB | **SERVES** 10
HANDS ON 30 min.
TOTAL 1 hr. 10 min.

- 1 Tbsp. olive oil
- 1½ cups farro
- 3 cups water
- ½ cup chopped onion
- ½ tsp. salt
- 1 lemon
- 2 cups small cauliflower florets
- 3 cloves garlic, minced
- 1½ tsp. ground turmeric
- ¼ tsp. black pepper
- 1 Tbsp. snipped fresh thyme

1. In a large heavy saucepan heat oil over medium-high. Add farro; cook and stir 5 to 6 minutes or until farro is toasted and has a nutty aroma. Stir in the water, onion, and salt. Bring to boiling; reduce heat. Simmer, covered, about 30 minutes or just until farro is tender.
2. Remove 2 tsp. zest and squeeze 3 Tbsp. juice from lemon. Stir lemon zest, cauliflower, garlic, turmeric, and pepper into farro mixture.
3. Cook, covered, over medium-high 4 minutes. Uncover; cook about 4 minutes more or until cauliflower is tender and liquid is absorbed, stirring occasionally. Stir in lemon juice and thyme.

PER SERVING (½ cup each) **CAL** 126, **FAT** 2 g (0 g sat. fat), **CHOL** 0 mg, **SODIUM** 125 mg, **CARB** 23 g (4 g fiber, 1 g sugars), **PRO** 4 g

Lemon Toasted Farro and Cauliflower Pilaf

Roasted Cauliflower
with Cheese Sauce

Roasted Cauliflower with Cheese Sauce

14 g CARB

SERVES 8
HANDS ON 35 min.
TOTAL 45 min.

Nonstick cooking spray
3 to 4 large heads cauliflower
¼ tsp. black pepper
1 Tbsp. olive oil
1 Tbsp. all-purpose flour
1 cup low-fat milk (1%)
½ cup shredded Gruyère cheese (2 oz.)
½ cup shredded Fontina cheese (2 oz.)
2 Tbsp. snipped fresh chives

1. Preheat oven to 425°F. Line two large baking sheets with foil; coat foil with cooking spray. Remove outer leaves from each head of cauliflower. For each, trim stem end, leaving core intact. Turn cauliflower head onto its side. Cut 1-inch slices from the widest section of the head (the core keeps the slices intact). You should have eight slices total. Reserve ends and loose pieces for another use.

2. Place cauliflower slices on the prepared baking sheets. Coat cauliflower with cooking spray and sprinkle with pepper. Roast 20 to 25 minutes or until tender and brown.

3. Meanwhile, for cheese sauce, in a medium saucepan heat oil over medium. Stir in flour; gradually stir in milk. Cook and stir until thick and bubbly. Cook and stir 1 minute more. Gradually add both cheeses, stirring until melted. Spoon cheese sauce over cauliflower and sprinkle with chives.

Tip Use the leftover cauliflower trimmings for mashed cauliflower, cauliflower soup, or as part of a fresh vegetable platter.

PER SERVING (1 slice cauliflower + 2 Tbsp. sauce each) **CAL** 150, **FAT** 8 g (3 g sat. fat), **CHOL** 10 mg, **SODIUM** 189 mg, **CARB** 14 g (5 g fiber, 6 g sugars), **PRO** 9 g

Pan-Roasted Brussels Sprouts

11 g CARB

SERVES 8
TOTAL 30 min.

2 lb. fresh Brussels sprouts
1 Tbsp. olive oil
7 cloves garlic, minced
3 Tbsp. butter
12 sprigs fresh thyme
1 large sprig fresh rosemary, halved
2 tsp. fennel seeds
½ tsp. salt
1 Tbsp. sherry vinegar or white wine vinegar

1. Trim stems and remove any wilted outer leaves from Brussels sprouts. Halve any large sprouts. In a large pot cook Brussels sprouts, uncovered, in a large amount of boiling lightly salted water 3 minutes; drain. Pat dry with paper towels.

2. In a 12-inch heavy skillet heat oil over medium. Add garlic; cook and stir 2 minutes. Add half of the butter, thyme, rosemary, fennel seeds, and salt. Increase heat to medium-high. Using tongs, carefully arrange half of the Brussels sprouts, cut sides down, in the skillet. Cook 4 to 6 minutes or until sprouts are well browned. Remove sprouts from skillet. Repeat with the remaining butter, thyme, rosemary, fennel seeds, salt, and Brussels sprouts. Return all sprouts to the skillet; Drizzle with vinegar; toss gently to coat.

PER SERVING (½ cup each) **CAL** 107, **FAT** 6 g (3 g sat. fat), **CHOL** 11 mg, **SODIUM** 184 mg, **CARB** 11 g (5 g fiber, 3 g sugars), **PRO** 4 g

Pan-Roasted Brussels Sprouts

**Roasted Cabbage
with Olive Tapenade**

*Roasted Cabbage
with Olive Tapenade*

Green Beans with Creamy Mushroom Sauce

11 g CARB

SERVES 8
HANDS ON 40 min.
TOTAL 40 min.

- 3 Tbsp. olive oil
- 1 cup thinly sliced shallots
- 1 lb. fresh green beans, trimmed
- 2 Tbsp. water
- ½ tsp. kosher salt
- ¼ tsp. black pepper
- 2 cups sliced fresh cremini mushrooms
- 1 Tbsp. fresh thyme leaves
- 2 to 3 cloves garlic, minced
- 1 Tbsp. all-purpose flour
- 1 cup low-fat milk (1%)
- ½ cup crumbled goat cheese (chèvre) (2 oz.)

1. In a 12-inch nonstick skillet heat 2 Tbsp. of the oil over medium-high. Add shallots; cook 4 to 5 minutes or until deep golden, stirring occasionally. Drain shallots on paper towels, reserving drippings in skillet.
2. Add green beans, the water, ¼ tsp. of the salt, and ⅛ tsp. of the pepper to reserved drippings. Cook, covered, over medium-high 2 minutes. Cook, uncovered, about 6 minutes more or until beans are crisp-tender and starting to blister, stirring occasionally. Transfer to a platter; keep warm.
3. For mushroom sauce, add the remaining 1 Tbsp. oil to skillet. Add mushrooms; cook and stir over medium 1 minute. Add thyme, garlic, and the remaining ¼ tsp. salt and ⅛ tsp. pepper. Cook about 2 minutes more or until mushrooms are golden, stirring frequently. Stir in flour; gradually stir in milk. Cook and stir until thick and bubbly. Cook and stir 2 minutes more. Pour mushroom sauce over beans and top with shallots and cheese.

PER SERVING *(¾ cup each)* **CAL** 119, **FAT** 7 g (2 g sat. fat), **CHOL** 5 mg, **SODIUM** 123 mg, **CARB** 11 g (3 g fiber, 5 g sugars), **PRO** 5 g

Roasted Cabbage with Olive Tapenade

10 g CARB

SERVES 8
HANDS ON 15 min.
TOTAL 50 min.

- 2 1¼- to 1¾-lb. heads red and/ or green cabbage, trimmed and cut lengthwise into 1-inch slices (discard cores)
- 1 shallot, halved and sliced
- 4 cloves garlic, minced
- ½ tsp. kosher salt
- ¼ tsp. freshly ground black pepper
- ¼ cup olive oil
- ¼ cup olive tapenade

1. Preheat oven to 425°F. Place cabbage in a 15×10-inch baking pan, overlapping slightly if necessary. Sprinkle with shallot, garlic, salt, and pepper and drizzle with oil.
2. Roast 35 to 40 minutes or until cabbage is tender, turning once. Top slices with olive tapenade.

PER SERVING *(1 slice each)* **CAL** 107, **FAT** 7 g (1 g sat. fat), **CHOL** 0 mg, **SODIUM** 206 mg, **CARB** 10 g (4 g fiber, 5 g sugars), **PRO** 2 g

QUICK TIP Thinly sliced sweet onion caramelizes beautifully and can be used instead of shallots.

Green Beans with
Creamy Mushroom Sauce

Herbed Green Beans,
Carrots, and Cranberries

Herbed Green Beans, Carrots, and Cranberries

18 g CARB

SERVES 6
HANDS ON 10 min.
TOTAL 15 min.

- 1 16- to 22-oz. pkg. frozen whole green beans
- 1½ cups julienned carrots
- ½ cup vegetable broth
- 3 Tbsp. butter
- 1 Tbsp. dried parsley
- 1 Tbsp. minced garlic
- 1 tsp. dried Italian seasoning, crushed
- ½ tsp. onion powder
- ½ cup dried cranberries
- ¼ tsp. salt
- ⅛ tsp. black pepper

1. In the cooking pot of a 6-qt. electric pressure cooker combine the first eight ingredients (through onion powder).
2. Cover with lid and lock securely. Select low pressure and set timer for 2 minutes (timer will start after cooker has come up to pressure). Quick-release pressure. Unlock and remove lid.
3. Stir in the remaining ingredients. Let stand 2 to 3 minutes or until cranberries are softened. Serve using a slotted spoon.

Tip To julienne carrots, peel and cut carrots in half lengthwise. Lay halves down on their flat sides and cut lengthwise into about ⅛-inch-thick strips. Stack strips a few at a time and cut into 2- to 3-inch lengths. For faster preparation, use packaged fresh julienned carrots.

Tip For crisper vegetables, reduce cooking time to 1 minute.

Stove-Top Pressure Cooker Directions Using a 4- to 6-qt. stove-top pressure cooker, prepare as directed in Step 1. Cover with lid and lock securely. Over high heat, bring cooker up to low (5 to 7 lb.) pressure. Reduce heat just enough to maintain steady pressure. Cook 2 minutes.

Spiced Maple Cranberry Sauce

Remove from heat. Quick-release pressure. Unlock and remove lid. Continue as directed.

PER SERVING (¾ cup each) **CAL** 129, **FAT** 6 g (4 g sat. fat), **CHOL** 15 mg, **SODIUM** 234 mg, **CARB** 18 g (4 g fiber, 10 g sugars), **PRO** 2 g

Spiced Maple Cranberry Sauce

14 g CARB

SERVES 12
HANDS ON 25 min.
TOTAL 55 min.

- 1 medium orange
- 1 12-oz. pkg. fresh or frozen cranberries
- ½ cup water
- ½ cup unsweetened applesauce
- ½ tsp. ground cinnamon
- ¼ tsp. ground ginger
- ¼ tsp. ground nutmeg
- ½ cup pure maple syrup

1. Remove 2 tsp. zest and squeeze ¼ cup juice from orange. In a medium saucepan combine orange juice and the next six ingredients (through nutmeg). Bring just to boiling; reduce heat. Simmer 15 minutes or until most of the cranberries pop and mixture is slightly thick, stirring occasionally. Remove from heat. Stir in maple syrup and orange zest. Cover and chill at least 30 minutes (sauce will thicken as it chills).
2. Pour half of the sauce into a blender or food processor; cover and blend or process until smooth. Stir pureed sauce into the remaining sauce.

PER SERVING (¼ cup each) **CAL** 55, **FAT** 0 g, **CHOL** 0 mg, **SODIUM** 3 mg, **CARB** 14 g (1 g fiber, 11 g sugars), **PRO** 0 g

Roasted Sweets and Greens

Roasted Sweets and Greens

29 g CARB

SERVES 10
HANDS ON 10 min.
TOTAL 45 min.

- 3 lb. sweet potatoes
- 2 Tbsp. olive oil
- ½ tsp. salt
- ½ tsp. black pepper
- ½ cup chopped hazelnuts
- 4 cloves garlic, minced
- 4 cups arugula
- ½ cup cider vinegar

1. Preheat oven to 400°F. Scrub sweet potatoes; pat dry. Halve potatoes lengthwise and cut into wedges. Place in a very large bowl. Drizzle with oil and sprinkle with salt and pepper; toss to coat. Spread in two 15×10-inch baking pans.

2. Roast about 30 minutes or until tender, turning once. Sprinkle with nuts and garlic. Roast 4 to 5 minutes more or until nuts are toasted. Top with arugula and drizzle with vinegar.

PER SERVING (about 5 wedges each) **CAL** 184, **FAT** 6 g (1 g sat. fat), **CHOL** 0 mg, **SODIUM** 194 mg, **CARB** 29 g (5 g fiber, 6 g sugars), **PRO** 3 g

Toasted Wild Rice Griddle Cakes

Toasted Wild Rice Griddle Cakes

10 g CARB

SERVES 18
TOTAL 1 hr. 15 min.

- 2 cups water
- 1 cup wild rice, rinsed and drained
- 3 Tbsp. butter
- 1 tsp. salt
- ¼ tsp. crushed red pepper
- ¾ cup finely chopped fennel
- ½ cup finely chopped red onion
- ½ cup coarsely shredded carrot
- 1¼ cups soft bread crumbs
- ⅓ cup grated Parmesan cheese
- 2 eggs, lightly beaten
- 2 Tbsp. canola oil
- ¼ cup sour cream
- 1 tsp. Dijon-style mustard
  Microgreens (optional)

1. In a medium heavy saucepan bring the water to boiling. Stir in rice; reduce heat. Simmer, covered, 40 to 50 minutes or just until rice begins to split; drain.

2. Add butter, salt, and crushed red pepper. Cook and stir over medium-high about 6 minutes or until rice is toasted and has a nutty aroma. Stir in fennel, onion, and carrot. Remove from heat. Stir in bread crumbs and cheese; cool 10 minutes. Stir in eggs until combined. If desired, cover and chill up to 6 hours. Stir before using.

3. For griddle cakes, in a 12-inch skillet heat oil over medium-high. Add 3 Tbsp. batter per cake, spreading to 3 inches. Cook 3 to 4 minutes or until bottoms are crisp and brown. Turn and cook 2 to 3 minutes more or until bottoms are brown. Keep warm in a

200°F oven while cooking remaining cakes. Add additional oil as needed to cook cakes.

4. In a small bowl stir together sour cream and mustard. Serve griddle cakes with sour cream mixture and, if desired, top with microgreens.

Tip Serve cakes with roasted meats or lightly dressed mixed greens. Top with chopped roasted red pepper, finely chopped red onion, thin shards of fennel, shredded Parmesan, and/or sour cream as an appetizer or party snack.

PER SERVING (1 griddle cake each) **CAL** 94, **FAT** 5 g (2 g sat. fat), **CHOL** 29 mg, **SODIUM** 207 mg, **CARB** 10 g (1 g fiber, 1 g sugars), **PRO** 3 g

Roasted Herb and Garlic
Smashed Potato Casserole

Roasted Herb and Garlic Smashed Potato Casserole

21 g
CARB

SERVES 8
HANDS ON 25 min.
TOTAL 1 hr. 15 min.

- 2 lb. tiny new red potatoes, quartered
- 3 Tbsp. olive oil
- 1 tsp. salt-free herb and garlic seasoning, such as Mrs. Dash
- ¼ tsp. black pepper
- 1 garlic bulb
- ½ tsp. kosher salt
- 1 cup plain fat-free Greek yogurt
- ¼ cup freshly grated Parmesan cheese
- ¼ cup snipped fresh parsley

1. Preheat oven to 325°F. Place potatoes in a 2-qt. rectangular baking dish. Drizzle with 1 Tbsp. of the oil and sprinkle with herb and garlic seasoning and pepper; toss to coat.
2. Cut off the top ½ inch of garlic bulb to expose ends of individual cloves. Leaving bulb whole, remove any loose, papery outer layers. Place bulb, cut end up, on a double thickness of foil. Drizzle bulb with 1 Tbsp. of the oil. Bring foil up around bulb and fold edges together to loosely enclose. Roast potatoes and garlic 50 to 60 minutes or until potatoes are tender, stirring potatoes once.
3. Remove garlic bulb from foil; let cool. Squeeze bulb from bottom of paper husk so cloves pop out. Add roasted garlic and any oil from foil packet, the remaining 1 Tbsp. oil, and salt to potatoes. Coarsely mash with a potato masher. Spread yogurt over potatoes and sprinkle with cheese and parsley.

PER SERVING (¾ cup each) **CAL** 157, **FAT** 6 g (1 g sat. fat), **CHOL** 3 mg, **SODIUM** 148 mg, **CARB** 21 g (2 g fiber, 3 g sugars), **PRO** 6 g

Arugula Fennel Salad

Arugula Fennel Salad

17 g
CARB

SERVES 8
TOTAL 25 min.

- ¼ cup white balsamic vinegar
- ¼ cup olive oil
- 1 clove garlic, minced
- ¼ tsp. salt
- ¼ tsp. freshly ground black pepper
- 1 bulb fennel, trimmed, halved, and cored
- 3 cups arugula
- 1 cup cubed fresh pineapple and/or peeled orange slices
- ½ cup golden raisins

1. In a large bowl whisk together the first five ingredients (through pepper). Using a mandoline or sharp chef's knife, thinly slice fennel. Add to bowl with the remaining ingredients. Toss gently to coat.

PER SERVING (1 cup each) **CAL** 127, **FAT** 7 g (1 g sat. fat), **CHOL** 0 mg, **SODIUM** 92 mg, **CARB** 17 g (2 g fiber, 12 g sugars), **PRO** 1 g

Balsamic Berry Vinaigrette Winter Salad

Wild Rice and Roasted Beet Salad

22g
CARB

SERVES 6
HANDS ON 30 min.
TOTAL 2 hr. 45 min.

- 1¼ to 1½ lb. beets with greens
- ⅔ cup wild rice
- 1⅔ cups water
- 1½ tsp. olive oil
- 2 Tbsp. finely chopped shallot
- 1 clove garlic, minced
- 2 Tbsp. red wine vinegar
- 1½ Tbsp. walnut oil
- 1 Tbsp. maple syrup
- ¼ tsp. salt
- ¼ tsp. black pepper
- 6 Tbsp. crumbled reduced-fat blue or feta cheese (1½ oz.)

1. Preheat oven to 425°F. Cut tops off beets; trim roots. Wrap each beet in foil. Place on a baking sheet. Chop 3 cups of the greens; set aside. (Reserve any remaining greens for another use.) Bake beets 1 to 1½ hours or until tender. Remove foil; let beets cool 15 minutes. To remove skins, wrap beets, one at a time, in paper towels; gently rub off skins. Chop beets.
2. Meanwhile, rinse wild rice in a fine-mesh sieve. In a small saucepan combine wild rice and the water. Bring to boiling; reduce heat. Simmer, covered, 40 to 50 minutes or until rice is tender and some of the grains split. Drain in a colander. Rinse with cold water until cooled. Drain again.
3. In a 10-inch skillet heat olive oil over medium. Add the 3 cups beet greens, the shallot, and garlic. Cook 3 to 5 minutes or until greens are wilted. Remove from heat; let cool.
4. For vinaigrette, in a screw-top jar combine the next five ingredients (through pepper). Cover; shake well.
5. In a serving bowl combine cooled wild rice, beet pieces, cooked greens, and pecans. Pour vinaigrette over salad; toss to coat. Top with cheese. Chill at least 30 minutes before serving.

PER SERVING (½ cup each) **CAL** 164, **FAT** 6 g (1 g sat. fat), **CHOL** 4 mg, **SODIUM** 245 mg, **CARB** 22 g (3 g fiber, 7 g sugars), **PRO** 6 g

Balsamic Berry Vinaigrette Winter Salad

8g
CARB

SERVES 8
TOTAL 20 min.

- ¼ cup balsamic vinegar
- 2 Tbsp. plain fat-free Greek yogurt
- 1 Tbsp. sugar-free strawberry preserves
- 1½ tsp. olive oil
- 1 tsp. Dijon-style mustard
- 1 clove garlic, minced
- ¼ tsp. kosher salt
- ⅛ tsp. black pepper
- 3 cups fresh baby spinach
- 3 cups torn romaine lettuce
- 1 small cooking apple, such as Braeburn or Gala, thinly sliced
- ½ cup crumbled blue, feta, or goat cheese (chèvre) (2 oz.)
- ½ cup pomegranate seeds
- ¼ cup chopped walnuts, toasted

1. For vinaigrette, in a small bowl whisk together the first eight ingredients (through pepper).
2. In an extra-large serving bowl combine the remaining ingredients. Drizzle with half of the vinaigrette; toss to coat. Pass the remaining vinaigrette.

PER SERVING (1 cup each) **CAL** 90, **FAT** 5 g (2 g sat. fat), **CHOL** 5 mg, **SODIUM** 144 mg, **CARB** 8 g (2 g fiber, 5 g sugars), **PRO** 3 g

**Wild Rice and
Roasted Beet Salad**

Roasted Beet and Pear Salad

17 g
CARB

SERVES	4
HANDS ON	15 min.
TOTAL	1 hr. 30 min.

8 oz. beets, without tops
    (3 small)
2 Tbsp. sherry vinegar
1 Tbsp. olive oil
½ tsp. Dijon-style mustard
¼ tsp. black pepper

⅛ tsp. salt
3 cups fresh baby arugula or
    spinach
2 cups sliced pears (2 medium)
3 Tbsp. shaved Gouda cheese
4 tsp. sliced almonds, toasted

1. Preheat oven to 425°F. Trim root ends from beets. Wrap each beet in foil and place in a 15×10-inch baking pan. Bake about 1 hour or until tender. Remove from foil; cool 15 minutes. Remove skins by wrapping beets, one at a time, in a paper towel and gently rubbing off the skins. Cut beets into bite-size pieces; let cool.

2. Meanwhile, for dressing, in a bowl whisk together the next five ingredients (through salt).

3. In a serving dish toss arugula with half of the dressing. Top with beets and pears; drizzle with the remaining dressing. Sprinkle with cheese and almonds.

PER SERVING *(1½ cups each)* **CAL** 123, **FAT** 6 g (1 g sat. fat), **CHOL** 4 mg, **SODIUM** 149 mg, **CARB** 17 g (4 g fiber, 11 g sugars), **PRO** 3 g

Citrus and Smoked
Almond Salad

Citrus and Smoked Almond Salad

7g CARB | **SERVES** 16
TOTAL 20 min.

¼ cup orange juice
3 Tbsp. lemon juice
¼ cup olive oil
½ tsp. kosher salt
¼ tsp. cracked black pepper
2 5-oz. pkg. torn mixed greens
2 oranges, peeled, halved, and sliced (1 cup)
2 grapefruit, peeled and sectioned (1 cup)
¾ cup pomegranate seeds
¾ cup smoked almonds, coarsely chopped

1. In a small bowl whisk together the first five ingredients (through pepper). In an extra-large bowl combine the remaining ingredients. Add dressing; toss gently to combine.

PER SERVING *(1 cup each)* **CAL** 91, **FAT** 7 g (1 g sat. fat), **CHOL** 0 mg, **SODIUM** 65 mg, **CARB** 7 g (2 g fiber, 3 g sugars), **PRO** 2 g

FRESH-BAKED
BREADS

6

Fill your home with the inviting scents of fresh-baked breads,

muffins, and scones. You don't need to resist these treats,

especially at the holidays, if you choose carb-careful recipes with

mindful portion sizes —just keep track of your carb count to make

room for them in your meal plan.

Whole Wheat Quick Bread

chopped (tip, p. *154*), into flour mixture. If desired, top batter in pan with additional jalapeño pepper and dried tomatoes. Bake as directed.

PER SERVING Same as original, except **CAL** 125, **FAT** 6 g, **SODIUM** 167 mg, **CARB** 16 g (4 g sugars)

PER SERVING WITH SUB Same as above, except **CAL** 123 cal., **CARB** 15 g (3 g sugars)

Parmesan-Herb Quick Bread

Prepare as directed, except stir ½ cup grated Parmesan cheese, ¼ cup snipped fresh parsley, 1 Tbsp. snipped fresh thyme, and 2 cloves garlic, minced, into flour mixture. Top batter in pan with ¼ cup additional grated Parmesan cheese. Bake as directed.

PER SERVING Same as original, except **CAL** 136, **FAT** 6 g, **CHOL** 16 mg, **SODIUM** 230 mg, **PRO** 5 g

PER SERVING WITH SUB Same as above, except **CAL** 134, (2 g sugars)

Chocolate Chip Quick Bread

Prepare as directed, except substitute unsweetened cocoa powder for ⅓ cup of the flour and stir ¼ cup miniature semisweet chocolate pieces into flour mixture. Increase sugar* to ¾ cup and add 1 tsp. vanilla to buttermilk mixture. Bake as directed.

PER SERVING Same as original, except **CAL** 164, **FAT** 7 g (2 g sat. fat), **CARB** 24 g (13 g sugars)

*Sugar Sub We do not recommend using a sugar sub for this variation.

Cranberry-Walnut Quick Bread

Prepare as directed, except stir ¼ cup each snipped dried cranberries and toasted, chopped walnuts; 1 to 2 tsp. orange zest; and 1 tsp. ground cinnamon into flour mixture. Increase sugar* to ¾ cup in buttermilk mixture. Bake as directed.

PER SERVING Same as original, except **CAL** 169, **FAT** 7 g, **CARB** 25 g (3 g fiber, 12 g sugars)

*Sugar Sub We do not recommend using a sugar sub for this variation.

Whole Wheat Quick Bread

15 g CARB

SERVES 16
HANDS ON 15 min.
TOTAL 2 hr.

Nonstick cooking spray
2 cups white whole wheat flour
½ cup ground flaxseed or flaxseed meal
2 tsp. baking powder
½ tsp. baking soda
¼ tsp. salt
1 egg, lightly beaten
1½ cups buttermilk
¼ cup vegetable oil
2 Tbsp. sugar*

1. Preheat oven to 350°F. Lightly coat a 9×5-inch loaf pan with cooking spray.
2. In a large bowl stir together the next five ingredients (through salt). Make a well in the center of the flour mixture. In a medium bowl combine the remaining ingredients. Add all at once to flour mixture. Stir just until moistened (batter should be lumpy). Spread batter in the prepared pan.
3. Bake 45 to 50 minutes or until a toothpick comes out clean. Cool in pan 10 minutes. Remove bread from pan; cool on a wire rack. If desired, wrap and store overnight before slicing.

PER SERVING *(1 slice each)* **CAL** 120, **FAT** 5 g (1 g sat. fat), **CHOL** 13 mg, **SODIUM** 166 mg, **CARB** 15 g (2 g fiber, 3 g sugars), **PRO** 4 g

*Sugar Sub Choose Splenda Sugar Blend. Follow package directions to use 2 Tbsp. equivalent.

PER SERVING WITH SUB Same as above, except **CAL** 118, **CARB** 14 g (2 g sugars)

Tomato-Jalapeño Quick Bread

Prepare as directed, except stir 2 cups chopped dried tomatoes (not oil-packed) and 1 fresh jalapeño chile pepper, seeded (if desired) and finely

Chocolate Chip

Parmesan-Herb

Tomato-Jalepeño

Cranberry-Walnut

Cranberry-Almond Bread

28 g CARB

SERVES 12
HANDS ON 25 min.
TOTAL 1 hr. 20 min.

- 1 cup whole bran cereal
- ¾ cup all-purpose flour
- ½ cup white whole wheat flour
- 1 tsp. baking powder
- ¼ tsp. baking soda
- ¼ tsp. salt
- 1 egg, lightly beaten
- 1 cup fat-free milk
- ½ cup packed brown sugar*
- 2 Tbsp. canola oil
- ½ tsp. almond extract
- ½ cup coarsely snipped dried cranberries
- ½ cup chopped almonds, toasted

1. Preheat oven to 350 F. Grease bottom and ½ inch up sides of an 8×4-inch loaf pan. In a large bowl stir together the first six ingredients (through salt). Make a well in the center of flour mixture.

2. In a medium bowl combine the next five ingredients (through almond extract). Add egg mixture all at once to flour mixture. Stir just until moistened (batter should be lumpy). Fold in cranberries and almonds. Spread batter in prepared loaf pan.

3. Bake 45 to 50 minutes or until a toothpick comes out clean. Cool in pan on a wire rack 10 minutes. Remove loaf from pan; cool completely on wire rack. Wrap and store loaf overnight before slicing.

PER SERVING *(1 slice each)* **CAL** 165, **FAT** 5 g (0 g sat. fat), **CHOL** 18 mg, **SODIUM** 137 mg, **CARB** 28 g (3 g fiber, 14 g sugars), **PRO** 4 g

*****Sugar Sub** We do not recommend using a sugar sub for this recipe.

Sweet and Savory Twist Bread

19 g
CARB

SERVES 24
HANDS ON 45 min.
TOTAL 1 hr. 45 min.

1 16-oz. loaf frozen whole wheat bread dough
1 16-oz. loaf frozen white bread dough
¼ cup chopped raisins
¼ cup chopped pecans
1 tsp. ground cinnamon
1 tsp. snipped fresh rosemary
½ tsp. crushed red pepper
½ tsp. cracked black pepper
1 egg, lightly beaten
1 Tbsp. water
Sea salt (optional)

1. Thaw dough according to package directions. Grease two 9×5-inch loaf pans. In a small bowl combine raisins, pecans, and cinnamon. Divide whole wheat dough in half. On a lightly floured surface roll half of the dough into a 9×8-inch rectangle. Sprinkle with half of the raisin mixture; press mixture into dough. Starting from a long side, roll dough into a rope; pinch edge to seal. Repeat with the remaining whole wheat dough and raisin mixture.

2. In another small bowl combine rosemary, crushed red pepper, and black pepper. Divide white dough in half. On a lightly floured surface roll half of the dough into a 9×8-inch rectangle. Sprinkle with half of the rosemary mixture; press mixture into dough. Starting from a long side, roll dough into a rope; pinch edge to seal. Repeat with the remaining white dough and rosemary mixture.

3. In a small bowl combine egg and the water; brush ropes with egg mixture. If desired, sprinkle the white dough ropes with sea salt. Twist one whole wheat rope and one white rope together to form a loaf, pressing ends together to seal. Repeat with the remaining two ropes. Place each loaf in a prepared loaf pan. Cover and let rise in a warm place until nearly double in size (about 30 minutes).

4. Preheat oven to 350°F. Bake 30 to 35 minutes or until bread sounds hollow when tapped. Remove from pans. Cool completely on a wire rack.

To Make Ahead Prepare as directed through Step 3, except after shaping loaves and placing in the prepared loaf pans, cover and chill up to 24 hours.

Before baking, let stand at room temperature 30 minutes. Bake and cool as directed.

PER SERVING (1 slice each) **CAL** 113, **FAT** 2 g (0 g sat. fat), **CHOL** 8 mg, **SODIUM** 197 mg, **CARB** 19 g (1 g fiber, 2 g sugars), **PRO** 4 g

Sweet ad Savory Twist Bread

Easy Oatmeal Bread

Toasted Millet No-Knead Whole Wheat Rolls

23 g
CARB

SERVES 24
HANDS ON 25 min.
TOTAL 2 hr. 15 min.

- 2 cups whole wheat flour
- 5 Tbsp. yellow cornmeal
- 2 pkg. active dry yeast
- 1½ tsp. salt
- ½ cup millet
- 2 cups milk
- ⅓ cup butter, cut up
- 2 eggs
- 3 Tbsp. molasses
- 2 to 2½ cups all-purpose flour
- 2 Tbsp. butter, melted

1. In a large bowl stir together whole wheat flour, 4 Tbsp. of the cornmeal, the yeast, and salt.
2. In a large saucepan cook millet over medium about 5 minutes or until toasted, stirring occasionally. Add milk and the ⅓ cup butter. Heat and stir just until warm (120°F to 130°F) and butter almost melts. Add milk mixture to yeast mixture; add eggs and molasses. Beat with a mixer on low 30 seconds, scraping bowl constantly. Beat on high 3 minutes. Stir in as much of the all-purpose flour as you can to make a soft, yet firm dough. Cover and let rise in a warm place until double in size (45 to 60 minutes).
3. Lightly grease a 13×9-inch baking pan. Punch dough down; turn out onto a floured surface. Using floured hands, press dough into an 11×7-inch rectangle. Cut into 24 pieces; transfer to the prepared pan. Cover and let rise in a warm place until double in size (30 to 40 minutes).
4. Preheat oven to 400°F. Brush rolls with the melted butter and sprinkle with the remaining 1 Tbsp. cornmeal. Bake about 25 minutes or until rolls are golden and sound hollow when lightly tapped. Cool in pan 10 minutes. Pull rolls apart and serve warm.

PER SERVING (1 roll each) **CAL** 151, **FAT** 5 g (3 g sat. fat), **CHOL** 26 mg, **SODIUM** 191 mg, **CARB** 23 g (2 g fiber, 3 g sugars), **PRO** 4 g

Easy Oatmeal Bread

29 g
CARB

SERVES 12
HANDS ON 25 min.
TOTAL 2 hr. 20 min.

- 1 cup warm fat-free milk (105°F to 115°F)
- ¼ cup honey or packed brown sugar
- 1 pkg. active dry yeast
- ½ tsp. salt
- 1¾ cups bread flour or all-purpose flour
- 1 egg
- 1 Tbsp. canola oil
- ¾ cup whole wheat flour
- ½ cup rolled oats
  Nonstick cooking spray
  Water (optional)

1. In a large bowl combine the first four ingredients (through salt), stirring to dissolve yeast. Let stand 5 minutes.
2. Add the bread flour, egg, and canola oil. Beat with a mixer on low to medium until combined. Beat on high 3 minutes, scraping bowl as needed.

Stir in whole wheat flour and oats. Cover and let rise in a warm place until double in size (45 to 60 minutes).
3. Lightly coat a 9×5-inch loaf pan with cooking spray. Stir dough and spoon into the prepared loaf pan. Cover and let rise in a warm place until double in size (about 30 minutes).
4. Preheat oven to 350°F. If desired, lightly brush loaf top with water and sprinkle with additional oats. Bake about 40 minutes or until bread is golden and sounds hollow when lightly tapped. Immediately remove from pan and cool on a wire rack.

PER SERVING (1 slice each) **CAL** 156, **FAT** 2 g (0 g sat. fat), **CHOL** 16 mg, **SODIUM** 113 mg, **CARB** 29 g (2 g fiber, 7 g sugars), **PRO** 5 g

Toasted Millet
No-Knead Whole
Wheat Rolls

QUICK TIP Molasses gives this loaf a hint of sweetness. Choose mild or full-flavored molasses depending on how deep and rich you want it to taste.

Molasses Buckwheat Loaf

Molasses Buckwheat Loaf

30 g CARB

SERVES 12
HANDS ON 35 min.
TOTAL 3 hr. 15 min.

- ½ cup warm water (105°F to 115°F)
- ¼ cup molasses
- 2 Tbsp. canola oil
- 1 pkg. active dry yeast
- ⅓ cup water
- 1¾ to 2¼ cups all-purpose flour
- 1 cup rye flour
- ½ cup buckwheat flour
- 1 tsp. salt
- 1 tsp. butter, melted

1. In a large bowl combine the first four ingredients (through yeast), stirring to dissolve yeast. Let stand 5 minutes. Add the ⅓ cup water. Stir in 1½ cups of the all-purpose flour and the next three ingredients (through salt) until nearly combined.

2. Turn dough out onto a lightly floured surface. Knead in enough of the remaining all-purpose flour to make a moderately soft dough that is smooth and elastic (5 to 7 minutes).

3. Shape dough into a ball. Place in a lightly greased bowl, turning to grease surface. Cover and let rise in a warm place until double in size (about 1½ hours).

4. Grease an 8×4-inch loaf pan. Punch dough down. Turn out onto a lightly floured surface and shape into a loaf. Using a sharp knife, make a few diagonal slashes in top. Place in prepared loaf pan. Cover and let rise in a warm place until nearly double in size (about 30 minutes).

5. Preheat oven to 350°F. Brush top of loaf with melted butter. Bake 40 to 45 minutes or until bread is a deep golden color and sounds hollow when lightly tapped. Immediately remove from pan and cool on a wire rack.

PER SERVING (1 slice each) **CAL** 162, **FAT** 3 g (0 g sat. fat), **CHOL** 1 mg, **SODIUM** 201 mg, **CARB** 30 g (4 g fiber, 5 g sugars), **PRO** 4 g

Nutty Honey Mini Rolls

Nutty Honey Mini Rolls

12 g CARB

SERVES 24
HANDS ON 25 min.
TOTAL 35 min.

- Nonstick cooking spray
- ¼ cup finely chopped toasted almonds
- 2 Tbsp. butter, softened
- 2 Tbsp. honey
- 1 tsp. ground cinnamon
- 1 8-oz. pkg. refrigerated crescent dough for recipes or refrigerated crescent rolls
- 1 recipe Honey Icing

1. Preheat oven to 375°F. Lightly coat twenty-four 1¾-inch muffin cups with cooking spray. Reserve 2 Tbsp. of the almonds. For filling, in a small bowl stir together the remaining 2 Tbsp. almonds, the butter, honey, and cinnamon.

2. Unroll crescent dough and cut into two equal rectangles. (If using regular crescent roll dough, pinch together seams of dough pieces to form two equal rectangles.)

3. Spread filling over dough rectangles, leaving about ¼ inch unfilled along the long sides. Starting from a long side, roll each dough rectangle into a spiral. Pinch to seal seams. Slice each spiral into 12 pieces. Place one piece, cut side up, in each prepared muffin cup.

4. Bake about 10 minutes or until golden. Cool in muffin cups 1 minute. Carefully remove rolls from muffin cups and arrange on a platter; cool slightly. Drizzle warm rolls with Honey Icing. Sprinkle with the reserved 2 Tbsp. almonds.

Honey Icing In a small bowl stir together 1 cup powdered sugar,* 2 Tbsp. honey, and 1 Tbsp. milk. If necessary, stir in additional milk, 1 tsp. at a time, to reach drizzling consistency.

PER SERVING (1 mini roll each) **CAL** 75, **FAT** 3 g (1 g sat. fat), **CHOL** 3 mg, **SODIUM** 84 mg, **CARB** 12 g (0 g fiber, 9 g sugars), **PRO** 1 g

***Sugar Sub** We do not recommend using a sugar sub for the powdered sugar in the icing.

Banana-Multigrain Streusel Muffins

27 g CARB

SERVES 20
HANDS ON 25 min.
TOTAL 50 min.

Nonstick cooking spray
1 cup all-purpose flour
½ cup whole wheat flour
2 Tbsp. flaxseed meal
2 tsp. baking powder
1 tsp. ground nutmeg
½ tsp. salt
¼ cup canola oil
¼ cup reduced-fat creamy peanut butter
½ cup packed brown sugar*
1 egg
1 cup whole bran cereal
1 cup mashed very ripe bananas (about 3 medium)
¼ cup light sour cream
1 Tbsp. vanilla
1 cup buttermilk or sour milk
1 recipe Streusel Crunch Topping

1. Preheat oven to 375°F. Line twenty to twenty-two 2½-inch muffin cups with paper bake cups. Lightly coat bake cups with cooking spray. (Or coat muffin cups with cooking spray.) In a bowl combine the next six ingredients (through salt).
2. In a large bowl combine oil and peanut butter. Beat with a mixer on medium 30 seconds. Gradually add brown sugar, beating until combined. Add egg, cereal, bananas, sour cream, and vanilla; beat just until combined. Alternately add flour mixture and buttermilk to banana mixture, beating on low after each addition just until combined.
3. Spoon batter into prepared muffin cups, filling each about three-fourths full. Sprinkle Streusel Crunch Topping over batter in muffin cups.
4. Bake about 20 minutes or until light brown and muffin tops spring back when lightly touched. Cool in muffin cups on a wire rack 5 minutes. Remove from muffin cups. Serve warm.

Streusel Crunch Topping In a bowl combine ¼ cup each all-purpose flour, rolled oats, and packed brown sugar;* add ¼ tsp. ground cinnamon. Add 3 Tbsp. canola oil; stir to combine.

***Sugar Sub** We do not recommend using a sugar sub for this recipe.

Tip To make 1 cup sour milk, place 1 tablespoon lemon juice or vinegar in a glass measuring cup. Add enough milk to make 1 cup total liquid; stir. Let stand 5 minutes before using.

To Store Store cooled muffins in an airtight container in the refrigerator up to 3 days. To reheat, wrap muffins in foil. Heat in a 350°F oven 12 to 15 minutes or until heated through.

PER SERVING *(1 muffin each)* **CAL** 181, **FAT** 7 g (1 g sat. fat), **CHOL** 11 mg, **SODIUM** 179 mg, **CARB** 27 g (3 g fiber, 13 g sugars), **PRO** 4 g

Orange-Date Pumpkin Bread

23 g CARB

SERVES 32
HANDS ON 25 min.
TOTAL 1 hr. 25 min.

2 cups all-purpose flour
1⅓ cups whole wheat flour
2 tsp. baking powder
1 tsp. ground nutmeg
½ tsp. baking soda
½ tsp. salt
1 orange
1 15-oz. can pumpkin
¾ cup sugar*
1 cup refrigerated or frozen egg product, thawed, or 4 eggs, lightly beaten
½ cup honey
⅓ cup canola oil
½ cup chopped walnuts or pecans, toasted
½ cup snipped pitted dates

1. Preheat oven to 350°F. Grease the bottom and ½ inch up the sides of two 8×4-inch loaf pans. In a large bowl stir together the first six ingredients (through salt).

Banana-Multigrain Streusel Muffins

Orange-Date Pumpkin Bread

Orange-Bacon Breakfast Toasts

2. Remove 1 tsp. zest and squeeze ⅓ cup juice from orange. In a medium bowl stir together orange zest and juice and the next five ingredients (through oil). Stir pumpkin mixture into flour mixture just until combined. Stir in walnuts and dates. Spoon mixture into the prepared loaf pans.
3. Bake about 50 minutes or until a toothpick inserted near centers comes out clean. Cool in pans 10 minutes. Remove from pans. Cool completely on wire racks. Wrap in foil or plastic wrap; store overnight before slicing.

PER SERVING (1 slice each) **CAL** 130, **FAT** 4 g (0 g sat. fat), **CHOL** 0 mg, **SODIUM** 102 mg, **CARB** 23 g (2 g fiber, 12 g sugars), **PRO** 3 g

***Sugar Sub** Choose Splenda Sugar Blend. Follow package directions to use ¾ cup equivalent.

PER SERVING WITH SUB Same as above, except **CAL** 123, **CARB** 20 g (9 g sugars)

Orange-Bacon Breakfast Toasts
Peel 1 orange; slice crosswise and cut up. Crisp-cook and crumble 2 slices bacon. Toast four scant ½-inch-thick slices Orange-Date Pumpkin Bread until light golden brown. Spread ¼ cup reduced-fat cream cheese (neufchatel) on the toasted slices. Top with orange pieces and bacon. Serve immediately. Makes 4 servings.

PER SERVING (1 slice) **CAL** 185, **FAT** 7 g (2 g sat. fat), **CHOL** 10 mg, **SODIUM** 95 mg, **CARB** 27 g (2 g fiber, 15 g sugars), **PRO** 5 g

Lemon-Poppy Seed Quick Bread

27 g **CARB**

SERVES 16
HANDS ON 20 min.
TOTAL 1 hr. 20 min.

2	cups all-purpose flour
1	cup sugar*
2	tsp. baking powder
½	tsp. salt
	lemon
1	egg, lightly beaten
1	cup milk
¼	cup vegetable oil
1	Tbsp. poppy seeds
2	Tbsp. sugar*
2	Tbsp. lemon juice
1	Tbsp. butter

1. Preheat oven to 350°F. Grease the bottom and ½ inch up the sides of an 8×4-inch loaf pan. In a large bowl stir together flour, the 1 cup sugar, the baking powder, and salt. Make a well in the center of the flour mixture.
2. Remove 1 Tbsp. zest and squeeze 2 Tbsp. juice from lemon. In a medium bowl combine lemon zest and juice, the egg, milk, oil, and poppy seeds. Add egg mixture all at once to flour mixture. Stir just until moistened (batter should be lumpy). Spread batter in prepared pan.
3. Bake 50 to 55 minutes or until a toothpick inserted near center comes out clean. Cool in pan on a wire rack 10 minutes.

4. Meanwhile, for lemon glaze, in a small saucepan combine the 2 Tbsp. sugar, 2 Tbsp. lemon juice, and the butter. Heat and stir over medium-low until butter is melted and sugar is dissolved. Remove bread from pan. Poke holes in the top of the warm loaf with a fork; slowly brush with lemon glaze. Cool completely on a wire rack. Wrap and store overnight before slicing.

*Sugar Sub We do not recommend using a sugar sub for this recipe.

PER SERVING (1 slice each) **CAL** 164, **FAT** 5 g (1 g sat. fat), **CHOL** 15 mg, **SODIUM** 152 mg, **CARB** 27 g (1 g fiber, 15 g sugars), **PRO** 3 g

Make It Mini Preheat oven to 350°F. Grease bottoms and halfway up sides of three 5¾×3-inch loaf pans. Prepare batter as directed. Spread batter evenly in prepared loaf pans. Bake about 40 minutes or until a toothpick inserted near the centers comes out clean. Cool in pans on a wire rack 10 minutes. Remove loaves from pans. Poke holes in the tops of the warm loaves with a fork; slowly brush with lemon glaze. Cool completely on wire racks. Makes 3 mini loaves (5 slices per loaf).

PER SERVING (1 slice) **CAL** 175, **FAT** 5 g fat (1 g sat. fat), **CHOL** 16 mg, **SODIUM** 129 mg, **CARB** 29 g (1 g fiber, 15 g sugars), **PRO** 3 g

To Make Ahead Wrap cooled loaf or mini loaves in foil or plastic wrap. Store in the refrigerator up to 1 week. Or place in freezer bag(s) or container(s) and freeze up to 3 months. If frozen, thaw overnight in the refrigerator.

Lemon-Poppy Seed Quick Bread

Triple-Spiced Pear Bread

Triple-Spiced Pear Bread

22 g
CARB

SERVES 28
HANDS ON 20 min.
TOTAL 1 hr. 20 min.

- 3 cups all-purpose flour
- 2 tsp. baking powder
- 1 tsp. ground ginger
- ½ tsp. baking soda
- ½ tsp. ground cinnamon
- ½ tsp. salt
- ¼ tsp. cardamom
- 1 cup buttermilk
- 1 cup milk
- 4 eggs, lightly beaten
- ½ cup melted butter
- ½ cup granulated sugar*
- ½ cup packed brown sugar*
- 1 tsp. vanilla
- 2 cups peeled and chopped pear
- ¾ cup regular rolled oats
- ¾ cup toasted walnuts, chopped

1. Preheat oven to 350°F. Grease the bottom and ½ inch up the sides of two 8×4-inch loaf pans. In a large bowl combine the first seven ingredients (through cardamom); make a well in the center.
2. In a medium bowl combine the next seven ingredients (through vanilla). Add to the flour mixture. Stir until just combined. Stir in pear, ½ cup of the oats, and the nuts. Spoon batter evenly into prepared pans. Sprinkle with the remaining ¼ cup oats.
3. Bake 50 to 60 minutes or until a toothpick inserted near centers comes out clean. (If necessary to prevent overbrowning, cover bread loosely with foil the last 15 minutes of baking.) Cool in pans on a wire rack 10 minutes. Remove from pans. Cool completely.

*Sugar Sub We do not recommend using sugar subs for this recipe.

Tip To toast walnuts, preheat oven to 350°F. Spread walnuts evenly on a baking pan. Bake 5 to 10 minutes or until toasted. Cool before chopping.

PER SERVING (*1 slice each*) **CAL** 161, **FAT** 7 g (3 g sat. fat), **CHOL** 37 mg, **SODIUM** 150 mg, **CARB** 22 g (1 g fiber, 10 g sugars), **PRO** 4 g

Savory Holiday
Corn Bread Muffins

Savory Holiday Corn Bread Muffins

16 g CARB

SERVES 8
HANDS ON 20 min.
TOTAL 40 min.

Nonstick cooking spray
½ cup all-purpose flour
¼ cup yellow cornmeal
1 Tbsp. sugar*
1¼ tsp. baking powder
2 eggs, lightly beaten
½ cup low-fat milk (1%)

⅓ cup refrigerated cooked turkey sausage crumbles
¼ cup shredded Gruyère or Swiss cheese (1 oz.)
¼ cup snipped dried cranberries
3 Tbsp. vegetable oil
4 tsp. light pancake syrup or honey

1. Preheat oven to 375°F. Line eight 2½-inch muffin cups with paper bake cups; coat paper cups with cooking spray.
2. In a medium bowl stir together the next four ingredients (through baking powder). In a small bowl combine the next six ingredients (through oil). Add milk mixture all at once to flour mixture. Stir just until moistened (batter should be lumpy). Spoon into prepared muffin cups.
3. Bake 15 to 17 minutes or until a toothpick inserted in centers comes out clean. Cool in muffin cups on a wire rack 5 minutes. Remove from muffin cups. Brush tops with syrup. Serve warm.

PER SERVING (1 muffin each) **CAL** 161, **FAT** 8 g (2 g sat. fat), **CHOL** 55 mg, **SODIUM** 179 mg, **CARB** 16 g (1 g fiber, 6 g sugars), **PRO** 5 g

*Sugar Sub Choose Splenda Sugar Blend. Follow package directions to use 1 Tbsp. equivalent.

PER SERVING WITH SUB Same as above, except **CAL** 159, 5 g sugars

Spiced Pumpkin Dinner Rolls

Spiced Pumpkin Dinner Rolls

22 g
CARB

SERVES 24
HANDS ON 30 min.
TOTAL 2 hr. 25 min.

4½ to 5 cups all-purpose flour
1 pkg. active dry yeast
1 cup warm fat-free milk (120°F to 130°F)
1 cup canned pumpkin
⅓ cup butter, melted
¼ cup packed brown sugar*
1¼ tsp. salt
1 tsp. ground cinnamon
1 tsp. ground coriander
¼ to ½ tsp. cayenne pepper
2 Tbsp. butter, melted
Sesame seeds (optional)

1. In a large bowl combine 2 cups of the flour and the yeast. In a medium bowl combine the next eight ingredients (through cayenne pepper). Add pumpkin mixture to flour mixture. Beat with a mixer on low 30 seconds, scraping bowl as needed. Beat on high 3 minutes, scraping bowl as needed. Stir in as much of the remaining flour as you can.
2. Turn dough out onto a lightly floured surface. Knead in enough of the remaining flour to make a moderately soft dough that is smooth and elastic (3 to 5 minutes). Place dough in a greased bowl, turning once to grease surface. Cover and let rise in a warm place until double in size (1 hour to 1½ hours).
3. Punch dough down. Turn out onto a lightly floured surface. Cover and let rest 10 minutes. Meanwhile, grease a 15×10-inch baking pan. With lightly floured hands, divide dough into 24 pieces; shape into balls. Arrange balls in the prepared pan. Cover and let rise in a warm place until nearly double in size (30 to 40 minutes).
4. Preheat oven to 400°F. Brush tops with the 2 Tbsp. melted butter. If desired, sprinkle with sesame seeds. Bake 15 to 20 minutes or until rolls are golden and sound hollow when lightly tapped. Remove rolls from pan; serve warm.

PER SERVING (1 roll each) **CAL** 133, **FAT** 4 g (2 g sat. fat), **CHOL** 10 mg, **SODIUM** 155 mg, **CARB** 22 g (1 g fiber, 3 g sugars), **PRO** 3 g

*Sugar Sub Choose Splenda Brown Sugar Blend. Follow package directions to use ¼ cup equivalent.

PER SERVING WITH SUB Same as above, except **CAL** 130, **CARB** 20 g (2 g sugars)

Scones with
Candied Lemons

Scones with Candied Lemons

30 g CARB

SERVES 12
HANDS ON 35 min.
TOTAL 4 hr. 10 min.

3 lemons
1 cup granulated sugar*
¾ cup water
1½ cups all-purpose flour
½ cup whole wheat flour
3 Tbsp. granulated sugar*
1½ tsp. baking powder
¼ tsp. baking soda
¼ tsp. salt
⅓ cup unsalted butter
2 eggs, lightly beaten
⅓ cup buttermilk
½ cup powdered sugar*
1 tsp. vanilla

1. Cut part of one lemon into six paper-thin slices; discard seeds. Remove zest and squeeze 2 Tbsp. juice from the remaining lemons. For candied lemons, in a 10-inch skillet heat lemon juice, the 1 cup granulated sugar, and the water over medium just until boiling, stirring until sugar is dissolved. Add lemon slices; reduce heat. Simmer gently about 15 minutes or until slightly translucent and rinds are softened, keeping slices in a single layer and turning occasionally. Remove from heat. Using tongs, transfer slices to a waxed paper-lined baking sheet; cool completely (about 1 hour). Discard syrup or reserve for another use. Cover and chill lemon slices 2 hours. Cut slices in half.
2. Preheat oven to 400°F. In a medium bowl stir together 2 Tbsp. of the lemon zest and the next six ingredients (through salt). Using a pastry blender, cut in butter until

mixture resembles coarse crumbs. Make a well in center of flour mixture.

3. In a small bowl combine eggs and buttermilk; add all at once to flour mixture. Stir with a fork just until moistened (some of the dough may look dry). Knead gently in bowl until dough comes together.

4. Turn dough out onto a lightly floured surface. Pat or lightly roll dough into an 8-inch circle. Brush with additional buttermilk. Cut into 12 wedges.

5. Place wedges 1 inch apart on a large baking sheet; top each wedge with a candied lemon half. Bake 12 to 14 minutes or until edges are light brown. Cool on baking sheet on a wire rack 10 minutes.

6. Meanwhile, for glaze, in a bowl stir together powdered sugar, vanilla, 1 Tbsp. additional buttermilk, and ½ tsp. of the lemon zest. Spoon over scones; let stand 5 minutes. Serve warm.

To Make Ahead The candied lemons can be made and chilled up to 2 days.

PER SERVING *(1 scone each)* **CAL** 187, **FAT** 6 g (4 g sat. fat), **CHOL** 45 mg, **SODIUM** 159 mg, **CARB** 30 g (1 g fiber, 13 g sugars), **PRO** 4 g

*Sugar Sub Choose Splenda Granular. Follow package directions to use 3 Tbsp. equivalent. We do not recommend using a sugar sub for the granulated sugar in the candied lemons and the powdered sugar in the glaze.

PER SERVING WITH SUB Same as above, except **CAL** 176, **CARB** 27 g (10 g sugars)

Ginger-Pear Scones

11 g CARB

SERVES 30
HANDS ON 30 min.
TOTAL 38 min.

- 2½ cups all-purpose flour
- 2 Tbsp. packed brown sugar*
- 1 Tbsp. baking powder
- 1 Tbsp. finely chopped crystallized ginger
- ½ tsp. freshly grated nutmeg or ¼ tsp. ground nutmeg

- ¼ tsp. salt
- ⅓ cup cold butter, cut up
- 1 cup finely chopped fresh pear
- 2 eggs, lightly beaten
- ⅔ cup heavy cream
- 1 recipe Spiced Butter

1. Preheat oven to 400°F. In a large bowl stir together the first six ingredients (through salt). Using a pastry blender, cut in butter until mixture resembles coarse crumbs. Stir in pear. Make a well in the center of flour mixture.

2. In a bowl combine eggs and cream. Add egg mixture to flour mixture. Using a fork, stir just until moistened.

3. Turn dough out onto a lightly floured surface. Knead dough by folding and gently pressing it 10 to 12 strokes or just until dough holds together. Divide dough in half. Lightly roll or pat each half of the dough into a 7-inch circle. Using a 2- to 2½-inch cutter, cut out scones. Reroll scraps to cut additional scones.

4. Place scones 2 inches apart on an ungreased baking sheet. Brush with additional heavy cream. If desired,

sprinkle with additional freshly grated nutmeg and/or chopped crystallized ginger.

5. Bake 8 to 12 minutes or until golden. Serve warm with Spiced Butter.

Spiced Butter In a bowl stir together 1 Tbsp. sugar,* ½ tsp. finely chopped crystallized ginger, ¼ tsp. freshly grated nutmeg or ⅛ tsp. ground nutmeg, and dash ground cinnamon. Stir in ½ cup softened butter until combined. Cover and chill until ready to serve.

PER SERVING *(1 scone each)* **CAL** 116, **FAT** 7 g (5 g sat. fat), **CHOL** 32 mg, **SODIUM** 103 mg, **CARB** 11 g (0 g fiber, 2 g sugars), **PRO** 2 g

*Sugar Sub Choose Splenda Brown Sugar Blend and Splenda Sugar Blend. Follow package directions to use 2 Tbsp. equivalent in dough and 1 Tbsp. equivalent in butter.

PER SERVING WITH SUB Same as above, except **CAL** 114, **CARB** 10 g (1 g sugars)

Ginger-Pear Scones

7

FESTIVE
ENDINGS

Whether it's an elegant cookie or a blockbuster chocolate cake,

the finish to a holiday meal calls for something sweet. This

generous assortment of desserts is slim on calories, carbohydrate,

and fat so you can indulge deliciously and stay within your

diabetes meal plan.

Chocolate Mint Crinkle Cookies (recipe, *p. 134*)

Salted Pistachio-White Chocolate Cookies (recipe, *p. 134*)

Chocolate-Orange Shortbread Tartlets (recipe, *p. 134*)

Vanilla Candy Cane Peppermint Bars

Cranberry Cheesecake Bars

15 g CARB

SERVES 24
HANDS ON 30 min.
TOTAL 6 hr. 15 min.

- 1 cup fresh or frozen cranberries
- ½ cup orange juice
- 2 Tbsp. granulated sugar*
  Nonstick cooking spray
- ½ cup regular rolled oats
- ½ cup whole wheat flour
- ¼ cup packed brown sugar*
- ¼ cup butter, melted
- 2 8-oz. pkg. reduced-fat cream cheese (neufchatel), softened
- ¾ cup granulated sugar*
- 1 tsp. vanilla
- ¼ cup fat-free milk
- 4 eggs, lightly beaten

1. In a small saucepan bring cranberries, orange juice, and the 2 Tbsp. granulated sugar to boiling; reduce heat. Simmer 10 to 15 minutes or until slightly thick. Cool slightly. Transfer to a food processor; cover and process until smooth. Strain through a fine-mesh sieve into a bowl (should have about ⅓ cup); discard solids. Wash processor bowl and blade.
2. Preheat oven to 350°F. Lightly coat a 13×9-inch baking pan with cooking spray. For crust, place oats in food processor; cover and process until coarsely ground. In a bowl combine ground oats, flour, brown sugar, and melted butter. Press onto bottom of the prepared pan (crust will be thin).
3. In a large bowl beat cream cheese, the ¾ cup granulated sugar, and vanilla with a mixer on medium until smooth. Beat in milk. Stir in eggs until combined.
4. Spread cream cheese mixture over crust. Drop cranberry mixture by teaspoons onto cream cheese mixture. Swirl slightly to marble.
5. Bake about 25 minutes or until edges are puffed and center is set. Cool in pan on a wire rack. Cover and chill 4 to 24 hours before serving. Cut into bars, wiping knife between cuts.

*Sugar Sub We do not recommend using sugar subs for this recipe.

PER SERVING *(1 bar each)* **CAL** 135, **FAT** 7 g (4 g sat. fat), **CHOL** 50 mg, **SODIUM** 92 mg, **CARB** 15 g (1 g fiber, 11 g sugars), **PRO** 3 g

Vanilla Candy Cane Peppermint Bars

22 g CARB

SERVES 16
HANDS ON 20 min.
TOTAL 1 hr. 40 min.

  Nonstick cooking spray
- ¾ cup sugar*
- ⅓ cup canola oil
- 1 egg
- 1 tsp. vanilla
- 1 cup all-purpose flour
- ½ tsp. baking powder
- ½ tsp. baking soda
- ¼ tsp. salt
- ⅓ cup crushed peppermint candies
- 3 oz. dark chocolate, melted

1. Preheat oven to 350°F. Line an 8-inch square baking pan with foil, extending foil over edges. Coat foil with cooking spray.
2. In a medium bowl beat sugar, oil, egg, and vanilla with a mixer on medium about 2 minutes or until slightly thick and pale yellow. Beat in flour, baking powder, baking soda, and salt just until combined. Stir in 2 Tbsp. of the peppermint candies. Spread batter in the prepared pan.
3. Bake 20 to 25 minutes or until edges are puffed and top is golden. Cool in pan on a wire rack. Using foil, lift uncut bars out of pan. Cut into bars.
4. Line a tray with parchment paper. Dip one corner of each bar into melted chocolate and place on the prepared tray. Sprinkle chocolate with the remaining peppermint candies. Let stand until set.

*Sugar Sub We do not recommend using a sugar sub for this recipe.

PER SERVING *(1 bar each)* **CAL** 155, **FAT** 7 g (1 g sat. fat), **CHOL** 12 mg, **SODIUM** 98 mg, **CARB** 22 g (1 g fiber, 14 g sugars), **PRO** 1 g

Recipes below pictured on pages 132-133

Chocolate-Orange Shortbread Tartlets

19 g CARB

SERVES 12
HANDS ON 45 min.
TOTAL 1 hr. 15 min.

- 1 cup all-purpose flour
- ¼ cup sugar*
- ¼ cup unsweetened dark cocoa powder
- ½ cup butter, cut up
- 1 5.3- to 6-oz. carton vanilla fat-free Greek yogurt
- 2 Tbsp. frozen 100% orange juice concentrate, thawed
- ½ of an 8-oz. container frozen light whipped topping, thawed
- 1 tsp. orange zest

1. Preheat oven to 350°F. Grease twenty-four 1¾-inch muffin cups. In a medium bowl stir together flour, sugar, and cocoa powder. Using a pastry blender, cut in butter until mixture resembles fine crumbs. Work mixture with your hands until it clings together (dough will be very dry to start).
2. Shape dough into 24 balls. Press balls onto bottoms and up the sides of the prepared muffin cups. Bake 12 to 15 minutes or just until firm. Cool in muffin cups 10 minutes. Run a thin sharp knife around the edge of each shortbread cup. Carefully remove cups from pan; cool on wire racks.
3. For filling, in a medium bowl combine yogurt and orange juice concentrate. Fold in whipped topping. Spoon or pipe filling into pastry cups. Sprinkle with orange zest.

PER SERVING *(2 tartlets each)* **CAL** 161, **FAT** 9 g (6 g sat. fat), **CHOL** 21 mg, **SODIUM** 87 mg, **CARB** 19 g (1 g fiber, 7 g sugars), **PRO** 3 g

*Sugar Sub Choose Splenda Sugar Blend. Follow package directions to use ¼ cup equivalent.

PER SERVING WITH SUB Same as above, except **CAL** 154, **CARB** 16 g (5 g sugars)

Chocolate Mint Crinkle Cookies

16 g CARB

SERVES 40
HANDS ON 50 min.
TOTAL 1 hr. 30 min.

- 4 oz. unsweetened chocolate, chopped
- 6 Tbsp. butter
- 1½ cups granulated sugar*
- 2 tsp. baking powder
- ¼ tsp. baking soda
- ¼ tsp. salt
- 3 eggs, lightly beaten
- ¼ cup plain fat-free Greek yogurt
- 1 tsp. vanilla
- ¼ tsp. mint (not peppermint) extract
- 1½ cups all-purpose flour
- ½ cup whole wheat flour
- ⅓ cup unsweetened cocoa powder
- ⅔ cup powdered sugar*

1. In a small saucepan cook and stir chocolate and butter over low until melted; cool slightly.
2. In a large bowl stir together the next four ingredients (through salt). Stir in chocolate mixture. Stir in eggs, yogurt, vanilla, and mint extract. In a small bowl stir together both flours and cocoa powder; sir into chocolate mixture until combined. Cover and chill dough until firm enough to handle (about 30 minutes).
3. Preheat oven to 350°F. Shape dough into 1½-inch balls. Roll balls in powdered sugar; place 2 inches apart on an ungreased cookie sheet. Bake about 8 minutes or just until edges are firm. Cool on cookie sheet 2 minutes. Remove; cool on a wire rack.

Tip For smaller cookies, prepare as directed, except shape dough into 1-inch balls. Bake about 7 minutes. Makes about 80 cookies (2 each).

*Sugar Sub We do not recommend using sugar subs for this recipe.

PER SERVING *(1 cookie each)* **CAL** 101, **FAT** 4 g (2 g sat. fat), **CHOL** 19 mg, **SODIUM** 67 mg, **CARB** 16 g (1 g fiber, 10 g sugars), **PRO** 2 g

Salted Pistachio-White Chocolate Cookies

12 g CARB

SERVES 45
HANDS ON 30 min.
TOTAL 1 hr. 20 min.

- ½ cup unsalted butter, softened
- ½ cup granulated sugar*
- ½ cup packed brown sugar*
- ¼ cup canola oil
- 1 tsp. baking soda
- ½ tsp. salt
- ½ cup refrigerated or frozen egg product, thawed, or 2 eggs
- 1 tsp. vanilla
- 2 cups all-purpose flour
- 1 cup salted, dry-roasted pistachio nuts, chopped
- 1 cup coarsely chopped white baking chocolate (6 oz.)

1. Preheat oven to 375°F. In a large bowl beat butter with a mixer on medium 30 seconds. Add the next five ingredients (through salt). Beat on medium about 2 minutes or until creamy, scraping bowl as needed. Beat in egg and vanilla. Beat in flour. Stir in ½ cup of the pistachios and ⅓ cup of the white chocolate.
2. Drop dough by tablespoons 2 inches apart onto an ungreased cookie sheet. Bake about 7 minutes or just until edges are brown. Cool on cookie sheet 2 minutes. Remove; cool on a wire rack.
3. In a small heavy saucepan cook and stir the remaining ⅔ cup white chocolate over low until melted and smooth. Pipe or drizzle melted chocolate onto cookies. Sprinkle with the remaining ½ cup pistachios. Let stand until set.

Tip To pipe the white chocolate, fill a small heavy resealable plastic bag with melted chocolate; snip a small hole in one corner of the bag. Squeeze the bag to pipe the chocolate onto cookies.

To Store Layer cookies between waxed paper in an airtight container. Store at room temperature up to 3 days or freeze up to 1 month.

PER SERVING (1 cookie each) CAL 105, FAT 6 g (2 g sat. fat), CHOL 6 mg, SODIUM 75 mg, CARB 12 g (0 g fiber, 7 g sugars), PRO 2 g

*Sugar Sub Choose Splenda Sugar Blend for the granulated sugar and Splenda Brown Sugar Blend for the brown sugar. Follow package directions to use ½ cup each equivalents.

PER SERVING WITH SUB Same as above, except CAL 98, CARB 9 g (5 g sugars)

Honey Lemon Almond Shortbread

19 g CARB

SERVES 12
HANDS ON 20 min.
TOTAL 35 min.

- 5 Tbsp. butter, melted
- ¼ cup honey
- 2 Tbsp. pure maple syrup
- 1 Tbsp. lemon zest
- ½ tsp. almond extract
- 1⅓ cups all-purpose flour
- ¾ tsp. sea salt
- ¼ cup sliced almonds

1. Preheat oven to 350°F. Line a cookie sheet with a silicone baking mat or parchment paper. In a medium bowl combine the first five ingredients (through almond extract).
2. In a small bowl stir together flour and salt. Add flour mixture to honey mixture; stir until combined. Cover and freeze 5 minutes.
3. Shape dough into 12 balls; place on the prepared cookie sheet. Press balls into 3×2-inch rectangles. Top with almonds.
4. Bake about 10 minutes or just until edges are golden. Cool on cookie sheet 5 minutes. Remove; cool on a wire rack. If desired, sprinkle with additional lemon zest.

To Store Layer cookies between waxed paper in an airtight container. Store at room temperature up to 2 days or freeze up to 1 month.

QUICK TIP Keep these crisp cookies in the freezer to pull out when you need a little gift. Stack them in a box with parchment and tissue papers and tie with a ribbon.

Honey Lemon Almond Shortbread

PER SERVING (1 cookie each) CAL 135, FAT 6 g (3 g sat. fat), CHOL 13 mg, SODIUM 139 mg, CARB 19 g (1 g fiber, 8 g sugars), PRO 2 g

White Chocolate Orange Crispy Trees

27 g
CARB

SERVES 16	
HANDS ON 25 min.	
TOTAL 1 hr. 30 min.	

Nonstick cooking spray
6 oz. white baking chocolate, chopped
3 Tbsp. butter (do not substitute)
½ of a 10-oz. pkg. (2½ cups) regular marshmallows or 4 cups miniature marshmallows
1 tsp. orange zest
Green gel, paste, or liquid food coloring (optional)
6 cups crisp rice cereal
4 oz. white baking chocolate, chopped
2 Tbsp. fat-free half-and-half
2 to 4 Tbsp. white and/or colored nonpareils or other small candies
1 to 1½ tsp. colored sugar* (optional)
16 long lollipop sticks (optional)

1. Lightly coat two 8- or 9-inch round cake pans with cooking spray. In a large saucepan melt the 6 oz. white chocolate and butter over low. Add marshmallows; stir constantly until completely melted (mixture may look too thick before the marshmallows melt completely). Remove from heat. Stir in orange zest and, if desired, green food coloring.
2. Add cereal. Stir until well coated. Divide cereal mixture between cake pans; pressing evenly with the back of a large spoon. Cool completely.
3. To make trees, carefully invert cereal rounds from pans onto a cutting board. Cut each round into eight wedges. If desired, make small cuts in the sides of the wedges to represent branches. If desired, bend tops of the wedges slightly to one side.
4. In a small bowl combine the 4 oz. white chocolate and half-and-half. Microwave, uncovered, on 50% power (medium) 1 minute. Stir until completely smooth. Pipe or drizzle over cookie wedges. Decorate with

White Chocolate
Orange Crispy Trees

nonpareils, small candies, and, if desired, colored sugar before the chocolate is set. If desired, pipe chocolate mixture into a small star at the top of each tree; sprinkle with yellow sugar. If desired, insert a lollipop stick into the wide base of each tree.

*Sugar Sub We do not recommend using a sugar sub for this recipe.

PER SERVING *(1 tree each)* **CAL** 183, **FAT** 8 g (6 g sat. fat), **CHOL** 6 mg, **SODIUM** 96 mg, **CARB** 27 g (0 g fiber, 18 g sugars), **PRO** 1 g

Salted Caramel Corn Cheesecake

17 g
CARB

SERVES	16
HANDS ON	20 min.
TOTAL	6 hr. 50 min.

Nonstick cooking spray
2 8-oz. pkg. reduced-fat cream cheese (neufchatel), softened
1 8-oz. pkg. fat-free cream cheese, softened
⅔ cup packed brown sugar*
2 tsp. vanilla
½ tsp. ground cinnamon
⅔ cup canned pumpkin
2 Tbsp. all-purpose flour
¾ cup refrigerated or frozen egg product, thawed, or 3 eggs, lightly beaten
1 cup Caramel Corn (recipe, *below*)
1 oz. bittersweet chocolate, melted

1. Preheat oven to 350°F. Lightly coat bottom and sides of a 9-inch springform pan with cooking spray. In a large bowl beat the next five ingredients (through cinnamon) with a mixer on medium to high until smooth. Beat in pumpkin and flour until smooth. Add eggs; beat on low just until combined. Pour into prepared pan, spreading to an even layer. Place in a shallow baking pan.
2. Bake about 45 minutes or until a 2½-inch area around outside edge appears set when gently shaken. Cool in pan on a wire rack 15 minutes. Using a small metal spatula, loosen edge of cheesecake from sides of pan; cool 30 minutes. Remove sides of pan; cool completely. Cover and chill 4 to 24 hours.
3. Top chilled cheesecake with Caramel Corn. Drizzle with melted chocolate. Let stand until chocolate is set. Cut into wedges.

Caramel Corn Preheat oven to 300°F. In a small saucepan combine 2 Tbsp. packed brown sugar,* 1 Tbsp. tub-style 60% to 70% vegetable oil spread, and ⅛ tsp. salt; cook and stir over medium just until boiling and sugar is dissolved.

Remove from the heat; stir in ½ tsp. vanilla. Place 3 cups air-popped popcorn in a shallow baking pan. Drizzle brown sugar mixture over popcorn; toss to coat. Bake, uncovered, 15 minutes, stirring once. Transfer to a large piece of foil; let cool 1 hour. Immediately place in an airtight container; cover and store at room temperature up to 2 days.

*Sugar Sub We do not recommend using a sugar sub for this recipe.

PER SERVING *(1 wedge each)* **CAL** 162, **FAT** 8 g (4 g sat. fat), **CHOL** 22 mg, **SODIUM** 231 mg, **CARB** 17 g (1 g fiber, 14 g sugars), **PRO** 6 g

Salted Caramel Corn Cheesecake

Maple-Date Cookies with
Cinnamon-Espresso Frosting

coffee powder until powder is dissolved. Add ¼ cup butter, cut up and softened; 1 cup powdered sugar;* and ¼ tsp. ground cinnamon. Beat with a mixer until smooth. Beat in 1 cup additional powdered sugar.* Beat in additional water, ½ tsp. at a time, to reach spreading consistency.

PER SERVING *(1 cookie each)* **CAL** 141, **FAT** 5 g (3 g sat. fat), **CHOL** 13 mg, **SODIUM** 73 mg, **CARB** 23 g (1 g fiber, 16 g sugars), **PRO** 1 g

***Sugar Sub** Choose Splenda Brown Sugar Blend. Follow package directions to use ½ cup brown sugar equivalent. We do not recommend a sugar sub for the powdered sugar in the frosting.

PER SERVING WITH SUB Same as above, except **CAL** 135, **CARB** 21 g (14 g sugars)

Cinnamon-Banana Cake

34 g
CARB

SERVES 16
HANDS ON 15 min.
TOTAL 1 hr. 10 min.

- 2 cups all-purpose flour
- ½ cup whole wheat pastry flour
- ½ cup granulated sugar*
- ½ cup packed brown sugar*
- 1¼ tsp. baking powder
- 1 tsp. ground cinnamon
- ½ tsp. baking soda
- ½ tsp. salt
- ¾ cup fat-free milk
- ⅔ cup mashed bananas (2 medium)
- ½ cup refrigerated or frozen egg product, thawed, or 2 eggs, lightly beaten
- ¼ cup canola oil
- 1 tsp. vanilla
- 3 oz. dark chocolate, chopped
- ¼ cup fat-free half-and-half

1. Preheat oven to 325°F. Generously grease and flour a 10-inch fluted tube pan. In a large bowl stir together the first eight ingredients (through salt).
2. In a medium bowl combine the next five ingredients (through vanilla). Add egg mixture all at once to flour mixture.

Maple-Date Cookies with Cinnamon-Espresso Frosting

23 g
CARB

SERVES 28
HANDS ON 30 min.
TOTAL 40 min.

- ½ cup butter, softened
- ½ cup packed brown sugar*
- ½ tsp. baking soda
  Dash salt
- ⅓ cup pure maple syrup
- 2 Tbsp. refrigerated or frozen egg product, thawed
- ½ tsp. vanilla
- 1⅔ cups all-purpose flour
- ⅓ cup whole wheat pastry flour
- ⅓ cup finely snipped pitted whole dates
- 1 recipe Cinnamon-Espresso Frosting

1. Preheat oven to 350°F. Lightly grease a cookie sheet or line with parchment paper. In a medium bowl beat butter with a mixer on medium 30 seconds. Add the next three ingredients (through salt). Beat until combined, scraping bowl as needed. Beat in the next three ingredients (through vanilla). Beat in both flours. Stir in dates.
2. Drop dough by teaspoons 2 inches apart onto the prepared cookie sheet; flatten slightly. Bake 8 to 10 minutes or until edges are light brown. Remove; cool on a wire rack.
3. Spread cookies with Cinnamon-Espresso Frosting. If desired, sprinkle with additional cinnamon and/or coffee powder.

Cinnamon-Espresso Frosting In a medium bowl stir together 2 tsp. hot water and 1 tsp. instant espresso

Beat with a mixer on medium to high 2 minutes. Spread batter in the prepared pan.

3. Bake 45 to 55 minutes or until a toothpick comes out clean. Cool in pan 10 minutes. Remove cake from pan; cool on a wire rack.

4. For ganache, in a small bowl microwave chocolate and half-and-half on 50% power (medium) 1 minute. Let stand 5 minutes. Stir until smooth. Let stand until slightly thickened. Spoon over cake.

PER SERVING (1 slice each) **CAL** 197, **FAT** 5 g (1 g sat. fat), **CHOL** 1 mg, **SODIUM** 177 mg, **CARB** 34 g (2 g fiber, 17 g sugars), **PRO** 4 g

*Sugar Sub Choose Splenda Sugar Blend for the granulated sugar and Splenda Brown Sugar Blend for the brown sugar. Follow package directions to use ½ cup each equivalents.

PER SERVING WITH SUB Same as at left, except **CAL** 177, **CARB** 27 g (10 g sugars)

Cinnamon-Banana Cake

Lemon Thumbprint Cookies

11g CARB

SERVES 48
HANDS ON 45 min.
TOTAL 2 hr. 10 min.

- 3 to 4 lemons
- ¾ cup butter, softened
- ½ cup granulated sugar*
- 1 egg yolk
- ⅔ cup granulated sugar*
- 2 egg whites
- 1 Tbsp. vanilla
- 2¼ cups all-purpose flour
- ¼ cup cornstarch
- ½ tsp. baking powder
- ½ tsp. salt
- 2 Tbsp. powdered sugar*

1. Remove zest and squeeze 6 Tbsp. juice from lemons. For lemon curd, in a medium bowl beat 2 Tbsp. of the butter and the ½ cup granulated sugar with a mixer on medium just until combined. Gradually beat in ¼ cup of the lemon juice and the egg yolk. Stir in 2 tsp. of the lemon zest (mixture may appear curdled).

2. Transfer mixture to a small saucepan. Cook and stir over low until smooth. Cook and stir over medium about 3 minutes or until slightly thick. Transfer to a bowl. Cover surface with plastic wrap and chill at least 1 hour (curd will thicken during chilling).

3. Preheat oven to 350°F. Line two large cookie sheets with parchment paper.

4. In a large bowl beat the remaining 10 Tbsp. butter and the ⅔ cup granulated sugar on medium until combined. Beat in egg whites, vanilla, 4 tsp. of the lemon zest, and the remaining 2 Tbsp. lemon juice (mixture may appear slightly curdled). In a small bowl stir together the next four ingredients (through salt). Add to butter mixture; beat just until combined. If necessary, chill dough 1 hour or until easy to handle.

5. Shape dough into 1-inch balls. Place 1 inch apart on prepared cookie sheets. Using your thumb, make an indentation in center of each ball.

6. Bake 12 to 14 minutes or until bottoms are very light brown. If cookie centers puff during baking, press with the back of a small spoon. Cool on cookie sheet 2 minutes. Remove; cool on wire racks. Sprinkle lightly with powdered sugar. Fill centers with lemon curd and sprinkle with additional lemon zest.

*Sugar Sub We do not recommend using sugar subs for this recipe.

To Store Place cookies in a single layer in an airtight container. Store in refrigerator up to 3 days.

PER SERVING *(1 cookie each)* **CAL** 73, **FAT** 3 g (2 g sat. fat), **CHOL** 11 mg, **SODIUM** 55 mg, **CARB** 11 g (0 g fiber, 5 g sugars), **PRO** 1 g

Almond Cannoli with Spiced Ricotta Filling

15 g CARB

SERVES 12
HANDS ON 45 min.
TOTAL 50 min.

- 2 egg whites
- ⅓ cup sugar*
- 3 Tbsp. all-purpose flour
- 3 Tbsp. ground almonds
- ⅛ tsp. salt
- 2 Tbsp. olive oil or almond oil
- ½ tsp. vanilla
- 1 8-oz. pkg. fat-free cream cheese, softened
- 4 oz. reduced-fat cream cheese (neufchatel), softened
- 3 Tbsp. honey
- ½ tsp. apple pie spice
- 1¼ cups light or part-skim ricotta cheese
- 2 Tbsp. chopped almonds, toasted

1. Preheat oven to 375°F. Line a large baking sheet with parchment paper. In a medium bowl beat egg whites with a mixer on medium to high about 20 seconds or until foamy. Add sugar; beat 1 minute. Sprinkle with flour, ground almonds, and salt; fold in gently. Drizzle with oil and vanilla; fold in gently.
2. Drop batter in 1½-Tbsp. portions about 6 inches apart onto prepared baking sheet; spread to 4-inch circles. Bake 5 to 7 minutes or until bottoms are light brown.
3. Immediately loosen cannoli from baking sheet. Turn over and wrap around metal cannoli cones or the straight metal handle of a whisk or honing steel; cool slightly. (If cannoli become too stiff to roll, return briefly to oven to soften.) While still warm, remove from cones and cool, seam sides down, on a wire rack.
4. For filling, in another bowl beat cream cheese on medium until smooth. Beat in honey and apple pie spice. Gently fold in ricotta cheese. Cover and chill until needed.
5. To serve, pipe or spoon filling into cannoli shells. Sprinkle ends with chopped almonds. Serve immediately.

*Sugar Sub We do not recommend using a sugar sub for this recipe.

Tip If you prefer, substitute 12 full-size or 24 miniature purchased cannoli shells for the homemade shells. Prepare filling and fill shells as directed.

To Make Ahead Prepare cannoli shells and filling as directed. Place shells in an airtight container and store at room temperature up to 3 days. Place filling in an airtight container and chill up to 3 days. To serve, let filling stand at room temperature 30 minutes to soften slightly. Fill shells as directed.

PER SERVING (1 filled cannoli each) **CAL** 150, **FAT** 7 g (2 g sat. fat), **CHOL** 16 mg, **SODIUM** 209 mg, **CARB** 15 g (0 g fiber, 12 g sugars), **PRO** 7 g

Apple Cake

Apple-Pomegranate Galette

22 g
CARB

SERVES 10
HANDS ON 30 min.
TOTAL 1 hr. 45 min.

- ¾ cup all-purpose flour
- ½ cup whole wheat flour
- 2 tsp. granulated sugar*
- ½ tsp. salt
- 3 Tbsp. butter, cut up
- 2 Tbsp. olive oil
- 2 to 3 Tbsp. cold water
- 2 Tbsp. honey
- 1 sprig fresh thyme
- 2 tsp. all-purpose flour
- 2 tsp. lemon juice
- 2 cups thinly sliced apples
- 1 egg white, lightly beaten
- 1 tsp. turbinado (raw) sugar*
  (optional)
- 2 Tbsp. pomegranate seeds or
  snipped dried cranberries
- 2 tsp. fresh thyme leaves

1. In a medium bowl stir together the first four ingredients (through salt). Using a pastry blender, cut in butter until pea size. Drizzle with oil and incorporate into flour mixture with your fingers. Sprinkle 1 Tbsp. of the cold water over part of the mixture; toss gently with a fork. Push moistened pastry to side of bowl. Repeat moistening flour mixture, gradually adding the cold water until mixture begins to come together. Gather pastry into a ball, kneading gently just until it holds together. Wrap in plastic wrap and chill 30 minutes.
2. Meanwhile, in a bowl combine honey and thyme sprig. Microwave 30 seconds; cool. Remove and discard thyme.
3. Preheat oven to 400°F. In a medium bowl combine infused honey, 2 tsp. flour, and lemon juice. Add apples; toss to coat.
4. On a large piece of lightly floured parchment paper roll pastry into a 12-inch circle. Slide paper with pastry onto a baking sheet. Mound apple mixture in center of pastry, leaving the outer 2 inches uncovered. Fold uncovered pastry over filling, pleating as needed. Lightly brush pastry with

Apple Cake

24 g
CARB

SERVES 16
HANDS ON 40 min.
TOTAL 1 hr. 15 min.

- Nonstick cooking spray
- 1 cup all-purpose flour
- ¾ cup whole wheat flour
- ⅔ cup sugar*
- 1½ tsp. baking soda
- 1 tsp. apple pie spice
- ¼ tsp. salt
- 1 egg, lightly beaten
- 1 egg white, lightly beaten
- 3 Tbsp. unsalted butter, melted
- 2½ Tbsp. canola oil
- 4 cups peeled and chopped
  apples
- 1 Tbsp. unsalted butter
- 1½ cups very thinly sliced apples
- 1 to 2 Tbsp. water
- 2 tsp. pure maple syrup
- ¾ cup frozen light whipped
  dessert topping, thawed
  (optional)

1. Preheat oven to 325°F. Coat a 9-inch square baking pan with cooking spray. In a bowl combine the next six ingredients (through salt). Stir in the next four ingredients (through oil). Stir in chopped apples. Press dough into prepared pan.
2. Bake about 45 minutes or until a toothpick inserted in center comes out clean. Cool in pan on a wire rack.
3. In a 10-inch nonstick skillet melt the 1 Tbsp. butter over medium. Add sliced apples; cook 8 to 10 minutes or until golden, adding 1 Tbsp. of the water every 4 minutes and stirring until it evaporates. Remove from heat; stir in syrup. Serve cake with apple mixture and, if desired, whipped topping.

*Sugar Sub We do not recommend using a sugar sub for this recipe.

PER SERVING *(1 square each)* **CAL** 151, **FAT** 6 g (2 g sat. fat), **CHOL** 19 mg, **SODIUM** 169 mg, **CARB** 24 g (2 g fiber, 13 g sugars), **PRO** 2 g

egg white and, if desired, sprinkle with turbinado sugar.

5. Bake about 35 minutes or until center is bubbly and pastry is brown. Cool 15 minutes. Sprinkle with the pomegranate seeds and thyme leaves.

PER SERVING (*1 wedge each*) **CAL** 149, **FAT** 6 g (3 g sat. fat), **CHOL** 9 mg, **SODIUM** 150 mg, **CARB** 22 g (2 g fiber, 8 g sugars), **PRO** 2 g

*****Sugar Sub** Choose Splenda Sugar Blend. Follow package directions to use 2 tsp. granulated sugar equivalent. We do not recommend using a sugar sub for the turbinado sugar.

PER SERVING WITH SUB Same as at left, except **CAL** 148

Apple-Pomegranate Galette

Pear-Cranberry Deep-Dish Pie

33 g **CARB**

SERVES	10
HANDS ON	40 min.
TOTAL	2 hr. 5 min.

⅓ cup sugar*
2 Tbsp. all-purpose flour
¼ tsp. ground nutmeg
¼ tsp. ground ginger
6 medium pears, cored and sliced (2 to 2½ lb. total)
1 cup fresh or thawed frozen cranberries
1 recipe Pastry
1 Tbsp. fat-free milk

1. Preheat oven to 375°F. In an extra-large bowl combine the first four ingredients (through ginger). Add pear slices and cranberries; toss gently to coat. Transfer to a 2-qt. round baking dish or casserole.

2. On a lightly floured surface flatten Pastry dough. Using a rolling pin, roll dough until ¼ inch thick. Using cookie cutters, cut small shapes from the pastry. Place dough cutouts on filling. Brush tops of dough cutouts with milk.

3. Place baking dish on a foil-lined baking sheet. Bake 55 to 60 minutes or until pear mixture is very bubbly. Cool pie about 30 minutes on a wire rack and serve warm. (Or cool completely.)

Pastry In a bowl stir together ¾ cup cake flour, ¼ cup whole wheat flour, and ¼ tsp. salt. Using a pastry blender, cut in ¼ cup chilled tub-style 60% to 70% vegetable oil spread until pieces are pea size. Sprinkle 1 Tbsp. cold water over part of the flour mixture; gently toss with a fork. Push moistened dough to the side of the bowl. Repeat moistening flour mixture, using 1 Tbsp. cold water at a time (3 to 4 Tbsp. total), until all flour mixture is moistened. Shape dough into a ball.

PER SERVING (⅔ cup each) **CAL** 169, **FAT** 4 g (1 g sat. fat), **CHOL** 0 mg, **SODIUM** 96 mg, **CARB** 33 g (4 g fiber, 16 g sugars), **PRO** 2 g

*****Sugar Sub** Choose Splenda Sugar Blend. Follow package directions to use ⅓ cup equivalent.

PER SERVING WITH SUB Same as above, except **CAL** 159, **CARB** 30 g (13 g sugars)

Pear-Cranberry
Deep-Dish Pie

All-American Apple Pies

27 g CARB

SERVES 4
HANDS ON 45 min.
TOTAL 1 hr. 5 min.

2   medium red apples or 4 very
     small red apples
¼   cup apple cider
4   Tbsp. water
1   Tbsp. all-purpose flour
2   tsp. sugar*
¼   tsp. apple pie spice
1   recipe Oil Pastry or 1 rolled
     refrigerated piecrust (½ of a
     15-oz. pkg.)
1   egg, lightly beaten
⅛   tsp. coarse sugar* (optional)
     Nonstick cooking spray

1. Preheat oven to 400°F. Cut two apples in half crosswise (or cut top third off four very small apples). Use a melon baller or small spoon to scoop out the flesh of each apple half, leaving an ⅛-inch-thick shell. Remove and discard seeds and core. Chop apple flesh into small pieces. In a small saucepan combine chopped apples, cider, 3 Tbsp. of the water, the flour, sugar, and apple pie spice. Cook and stir over medium 3 to 5 minutes or until apples are softened and liquid is thickened and bubbly. Return filling to apple shells.

2. Roll Oil Pastry into a large circle, about 10 inches in diameter. Using a 3½-inch cookie cutter, cut four circles from pastry. Discard trimmings or save for another use. Cut pastry circles into ¼-inch-thick strips. Lay strips in lattice over the top of the apples. (Or place full pastry circles over the tops of the apples and crimp edges.) In a bowl whisk together the egg and remaining 1 Tbsp. water. Brush egg mixture over pastry and, if desired, sprinkle with coarse sugar.

3. Line a 15×10-inch baking pan with foil; coat foil with cooking spray. Place pies on prepared baking sheet. If using very small apples, place apple tops on foil next to pies.

4. Bake 20 to 25 minutes or until apples are soft, filling is bubbly, and crust is golden. Serve immediately.

Oil Pastry In a medium bowl stir together 1⅓ cups all-purpose flour and ¼ tsp. salt. Add ¼ cup vegetable oil and ¼ cup milk to flour mixture. Stir lightly with a fork until combined (dough will appear crumbly). Gather flour mixture into a ball, kneading gently until it holds together.

*__Sugar Sub__ We do not recommend using a sugar subs for this recipe.

PER SERVING (1 apple pie each) **CAL** 131, **FAT** 3 g (0 g sat. fat), **CHOL** 0 mg, **SODIUM** 30 mg, **CARB** 27 g (3 g fiber, 16 g sugars), **PRO** 1 g

Spoonable Pumpkin Pie

Spoonable Pumpkin Pie

Tip This spoonable dessert is best served in small bowls with spoons.

PER SERVING (¾ cup each) **CAL** 163, **FAT** 9 g (4 g sat. fat), **CHOL** 14 mg, **SODIUM** 300 mg, **CARB** 18 g (1 g fiber, 7 g sugars), **PRO** 3 g

Chocolate Tiramisu Cake Roll

27 g
CARB

SERVES 12
HANDS ON 40 min.
TOTAL 3 hr. 55 min.

- ⅓ cup all-purpose flour
- ¼ cup unsweetened cocoa powder
- 1 oz. dark chocolate, grated
- ¼ tsp. baking soda
- ¼ tsp. salt
- 4 eggs, room temperature
- 1 Tbsp. instant espresso coffee powder
- 1 cup sugar*
- ¼ cup water
- 1 Tbsp. coffee liqueur or cooled strong coffee
- 1 recipe Cream Cheese Filling
- 1½ oz. dark chocolate, melted (optional)

1. Preheat oven to 375°F. Grease a 15×10-inch baking pan. Line bottom of pan with parchment paper; grease and lightly flour parchment. In a small bowl stir together the first five ingredients (through salt).
2. In a large bowl beat eggs and espresso powder with a mixer on high 5 minutes. Gradually add ¾ cup of the sugar, beating about 5 minutes more or until thick. Fold in flour mixture. Spread batter in prepared pan.
3. Bake about 15 minutes or until top springs back when lightly touched. Immediately loosen edges of cake from pan and turn cake out onto a towel sprinkled with additional cocoa powder. Carefully peel off parchment. Starting from a short side, roll towel and cake into a spiral. Cool on a wire rack 1 hour.
4. For syrup, in a small saucepan combine the remaining ¼ cup sugar

Spoonable Pumpkin Pie

18 g
CARB

SERVES 18
HANDS ON 20 min.
TOTAL 4 hr. 30 min.

- 1½ cups graham cracker crumbs
- ⅓ cup light butter, melted
- 1 15-oz. can pumpkin
- 1 8-oz. pkg. reduced-fat cream cheese (neufchatel) or whipped cream cheese spread, softened
- 3 1-oz. pkg. fat-free, sugar-free, reduced-calorie vanilla instant pudding mix
- 1½ tsp. pumpkin pie spice
- 1½ tsp. vanilla
- 2½ cups fat-free milk
- 1 8-oz. container frozen light whipped dessert topping, thawed
- ½ cup chopped pecans, toasted

1. Preheat oven to 350°F. For crust, in a food processor combine graham crackers and melted butter. Cover and pulse until well mixed. Press mixture onto the bottom of a 3-qt. rectangular baking dish. Bake about 10 minutes or just until golden; cool.
2. In a large bowl beat pumpkin, cream cheese, pudding mix, 1 tsp. of the pumpkin pie spice, and the vanilla with a mixer on medium to high until combined. Gradually add milk, beating on low to medium about 3 minutes or until smooth. Spread mixture over crust.
3. In the same bowl fold together whipped topping and the remaining ½ tsp. pumpkin pie spice; spread over pumpkin layer. Sprinkle with pecans. Cover and chill 4 to 8 hours before serving.

and the water. Bring to boiling over medium, stirring to dissolve sugar. Remove from heat. Stir in liqueur; cool.

5. Unroll cake; remove towel. Brush cake with syrup. Spread with Cream Cheese Filling to within 1 inch of the edges. Roll up cake; trim ends. Cover and chill 2 to 24 hours. If desired, drizzle with melted chocolate.

Cream Cheese Filling In a medium bowl beat 4 oz. softened light cream cheese spread with a mixer on medium until smooth. Gradually beat in 2 Tbsp. fat-free milk. Beat in 2 Tbsp. unsweetened cocoa powder and 1½ Tbsp. coffee liqueur or cooled strong coffee. Fold in 1 cup frozen light whipped dessert topping, thawed. Use immediately or cover and chill up to 24 hours.

PER SERVING *(1 slice each)* **CAL** 171, **FAT** 6 g (3 g sat. fat), **CHOL** 69 mg, **SODIUM** 148 mg, **CARB** 27 g (1 g fiber, 21 g sugars), **PRO** 4 g

*Sugar Sub Choose Splenda Sugar Blend. Follow package directions to use 1 cup equivalent, dividing it between the cake and syrup.

PER SERVING WITH SUB Same as at left, except **CAL** 146, **CARB** 18 g (12 g sugars)

Chocolate Tiramisu Cake Roll

QUICK TIP For a frosty look on the cranberries, pull them from the freezer just before topping and serving the cake.

Chocolate-Cranberry Cake with Almond Filling

Chocolate-Cranberry Cake with Almond Filling

30 g CARB

SERVES 16
HANDS ON 30 min.
TOTAL 2 hr.

- 1⅓ cups all-purpose flour
- ⅓ cup whole wheat pastry flour or whole wheat flour
- ¾ cup granulated sugar*
- ⅔ cup unsweetened cocoa powder
- 1½ tsp. baking powder
- ½ tsp. baking soda
- ¼ tsp. salt
- 1 cup water
- ¾ cup fresh cranberries
- ½ cup refrigerated pasteurized egg whites
- ¼ cup canola oil
- 1 recipe Almond Cream Filling
- 1 recipe Chocolate Glaze
- ½ cup frozen whole cranberries (optional)

1. Preheat oven to 350°F. Grease and lightly flour two 9-inch round cake pans. In a large bowl combine the first seven ingredients (through salt). In a blender combine the next four ingredients (through oil). Cover and blend until smooth. Add to flour mixture. Whisk until well combined. Divide batter between prepared pans, spreading evenly.

2. Bake 15 to 18 minutes or until a toothpick comes out clean. Cool cakes in pans on a wire rack 10 minutes. Remove cakes from pans; cool completely on wire rack.

3. To assemble, place one cake on a platter. Spoon Almond Cream Filling over cake, spreading evenly. Add second cake. Spoon and spread Chocolate Glaze over cake, allowing some of the glaze to run down the sides. Let cake stand 15 to 20 minutes or until glaze is set. If desired, top cake with frozen cranberries.

Almond Cream Filling In a medium bowl gently fold ½ cup powdered sugar* into ¾ cup whipped cream cheese spread until combined. (Do not overmix.) Gently stir in ¼ cup finely chopped almonds.

Chocolate Glaze In a small bowl combine 2 oz. bittersweet chocolate, chopped, and 3 Tbsp. fat-free half-and-half. Microwave, uncovered, on 50% power (medium) 1 minute. Add honey; do not stir. Let stand 5 minutes. Stir until completely smooth and slightly thickened.

PER SERVING (1 slice each) **CAL** 192, **FAT** 8 g (3 g sat. fat), **CHOL** 6 mg, **SODIUM** 169 mg, **CARB** 30 g (2 g fiber, 16 g sugars), **PRO** 4 g

*****Sugar Sub** Choose Splenda Sugar Blend. Follow package directions to use ¾ cup granulated sugar equivalent. We do not recommend using a sugar sub for the powdered sugar in the filling.

PER SERVING WITH SUB Same as above, except **CAL** 178, **CARB** 25 g (11 g sugars)

Jeweled Ginger Mini Cakes

30 g CARB

SERVES 12
HANDS ON 25 min.
TOTAL 50 min.

Nonstick cooking spray
- 1 cup all-purpose flour
- ½ cup whole wheat pastry flour or whole wheat flour
- 2 Tbsp. sugar*
- 1½ tsp. apple pie spice
- 1¼ tsp. baking powder
- ¼ tsp. baking soda
- ⅛ tsp. salt
- ¾ cup unsweetened applesauce
- ½ cup refrigerated or frozen egg product, thawed, or 2 eggs, lightly beaten
- ⅓ cup mild-flavor molasses
- ¼ cup canola oil
- ⅓ cup chopped mixed candied fruit (such as red and green cherries) and/or chopped candied citrus peels
- 1 recipe Maple Cream Cheese Frosting
  Freshly grated nutmeg (optional)

1. Preheat oven to 350°F. Line twelve 2½-inch muffin cups with paper bake cups; lightly coat cups with cooking spray. In a large bowl combine the next seven ingredients (through salt). In a medium bowl whisk together the next four ingredients (through oil). Add applesauce mixture to flour mixture; stir just until combined. Fold in candied fruit and/or citrus peel. Spoon batter into the prepared muffin cups, filling each about two-thirds full.
2. Bake 15 to 20 minutes or until a toothpick comes out clean. Cool in muffin cups 5 minutes. Remove; cool completely on a wire rack.
3. Spread or pipe Maple Cream Cheese Frosting on cupcakes. If desired, sprinkle with freshly grated nutmeg.

Maple Cream Cheese Frosting
In a medium bowl beat ⅓ cup softened light tub-style cream cheese, 2 Tbsp. pure maple syrup, and ½ tsp. vanilla with a mixer on medium until well combined. In another medium bowl beat ¼ cup heavy cream with the mixer on medium until soft peaks form (tips curl). Gently fold about one-third of the whipped cream into cream cheese mixture. Add all cream cheese mixture to remaining whipped cream; gently fold until combined.

*Sugar Sub We do not recommend using a sugar sub for this recipe.

PER SERVING *(1 mini cake each)* **CAL** 203, **FAT** 8 g (2 g sat. fat), **CHOL** 10 mg, **SODIUM** 162 mg, **CARB** 30 g (1 g fiber, 16 g sugars), **PRO** 3 g

White Chocolate Pudding Cake

31 g CARB

SERVES 12
HANDS ON 55 min.
TOTAL 1 hr. 30 min.

- 1 recipe White Chocolate Pudding
- 1 cup all-purpose flour
- 1 tsp. baking powder
- ¼ tsp. salt
- 2 eggs, room temperature
- ⅔ cup sugar*
- ½ cup fat-free milk
- 2 Tbsp. butter
- 1 tsp. vanilla
- ⅓ cup finely chopped raw macadamia nuts
- 2 Tbsp. sugar*

1. Prepare White Chocolate Pudding; chill overnight.
2. Preheat oven to 350°F. Line a 9-inch round cake pan with nonstick foil, extending foil over edges. In a bowl stir together the next three ingredients (through salt).
3. In a medium bowl beat eggs with a mixer on high about 4 minutes or until thick. Gradually add the ⅔ cup sugar, beating on medium 4 to 5 minutes or until light and fluffy. Beat in flour mixture just until combined.
4. In a small saucepan cook and stir milk and butter over medium until butter is melted. Add milk mixture and vanilla to egg mixture, beating until combined. Spread batter in the prepared pan.

White Chocolate Pudding Cake

5. Bake 20 minutes. Sprinkle with nuts and the 2 Tbsp. sugar. Bake 5 to 10 minutes more or until a toothpick comes out clean. Cool in pan on a wire rack 10 minutes. Using foil, lift cake out of pan. Remove foil; cool cake completely on a wire rack.

6. Using a long serrated knife, cut cake in half horizontally. Spread cut side of cake bottom with White Chocolate Pudding. Add cake top, nut side up.

White Chocolate Pudding In a medium saucepan stir together 3 Tbsp. sugar* and 4 tsp. cornstarch. Stir in 1¼ cups fat-free milk. Cook and stir over medium until thickened and bubbly; reduce heat. Cook and stir 2 minutes more. Remove from heat. Gradually stir about ½ cup of the hot mixture into 2 lightly beaten egg yolks. Add yolk mixture to saucepan. Bring to a gentle boil, stirring constantly; reduce heat. Cook and stir 2 minutes more. Remove from heat. Stir in 2 oz. white baking chocolate, chopped; 1 Tbsp. lemon juice; and 1 tsp. each butter and vanilla. Place pan in an extra-large bowl half-filled with ice water; stir to cool. Transfer pudding to a bowl; cover surface with plastic wrap. Chill.

*Sugar Sub We do not recommend using a sugar sub for this recipe.

PER SERVING (1 slice each) **CAL** 213, **FAT** 8 g (3 g sat. fat), **CHOL** 69 mg, **SODIUM** 152 mg, **CARB** 31 g (1 g fiber, 21 g sugars), **PRO** 4 g

**Frozen Wintery
Peanut Butter Bars**

Frozen Wintery
Peanut Butter Bars

22 g
CARB

SERVES 18
HANDS ON 15 min.
TOTAL 1 hr.

1½ qt. fat-free vanilla frozen yogurt
3 medium bananas, chopped
⅔ cup unsalted peanuts, toasted and coarsely chopped
⅓ cup miniature semisweet chocolate pieces
Nonstick cooking spray

⅓ cup natural creamy peanut butter

1. Allow frozen yogurt to stand at room temperature about 15 minutes or until slightly softened; stir gently. In a bowl stir together softened frozen yogurt, bananas, half of the peanuts, and half of the chocolate pieces.

2. Spread yogurt mixture in the bottom of a 13×9-inch baking pan. Sprinkle with the remaining peanuts and chocolate pieces.

3. Coat a small bowl with cooking spray; add peanut butter. Microwave 30 seconds; stir until smooth. Drizzle peanut butter over yogurt mixture. Cover and freeze at least 30 minutes before serving. Cut into bars.

Tip To toast peanuts, spread them in a shallow baking pan lined with parchment paper. Bake in a 350°F oven 5 to 10 minutes or until golden, shaking pan once or twice.

PER SERVING (*1 bar each*) **CAL** 159, **FAT** 6 g (1 g sat. fat), **CHOL** 0 mg, **SODIUM** 53 mg, **CARB** 22 g (1 g fiber, 14 g sugars), **PRO** 5 g

Frozen Espresso Peppermint Bombe

29 g
CARB

SERVES 10
HANDS ON 20 min.
TOTAL 28 hr. 20 min.

- 4 cups light chocolate ice cream, softened
- ½ tsp. peppermint extract
- ¾ cup finely crushed chocolate graham crackers (10 squares)
- 2 Tbsp. butter, melted
- 1½ tsp. instant espresso coffee powder
- 2 tsp. water
- 1 8-oz. container frozen light whipped dessert topping, thawed
- 4 small peppermint or sugar-free peppermint hard candies, crushed
  Coarsely ground coffee beans (optional)

1. Line a 1-qt. bowl with plastic wrap. Freeze 30 minutes.
2. For filling, in a bowl stir together softened ice cream and peppermint extract just until combined. Spoon into prepared bowl, packing firmly. Cover and freeze 4 hours or until firm.
3. In bowl stir together graham cracker crumbs and melted butter until evenly coated. Sprinkle over ice cream; press to pack very firmly. Cover and freeze 24 hours or until firm.
4. In a bowl dissolve espresso powder in water. Gently fold espresso into whipped topping until just combined (be careful not to overmix; there may be some streaks left). Cover and chill until ready to serve.
5. Unmold bombe onto a platter, loosening with a thin spatula if necessary. Remove and discard plastic wrap.

6. Spoon espresso mixture into a pastry bag fitted with a star tip. Quickly pipe espresso mixture over the bombe to completely cover. Sprinkle with crushed peppermints and, if desired, ground coffee beans. Freeze at least 1 hour before serving.

PER SERVING (*1 slice each*) **CAL** 193, **FAT** 8 g (6 g sat. fat), **CHOL** 14 mg, **SODIUM** 108 mg, **CARB** 29 g (1 g fiber, 16 g sugars), **PRO** 2 g

Frozen Espresso Peppermint Bombe

RECIPE GUIDE

High-standards testing

This seal assures you that every recipe in *Diabetic Living® Holiday Cooking* has been tested by the Better Homes & Gardens® Diabetic Living® Test Kitchen. This means each recipe is practical, reliable, and meets our high standards of taste appeal.

Inside Our Recipes

Precise serving sizes (listed below the recipe title) help you to manage portions.

Ingredients listed as optional are not included in the per-serving nutrition analysis.

When kitchen basics such as ice, salt, black pepper, and nonstick cooking spray are not listed in the ingredients list, they are italicized in the directions.

Ingredients
- Tub-style vegetable oil spread refers to 60% to 70% vegetable oil product.
- Lean ground beef refers to 95% or leaner ground beef.

Nutrition Information

Nutrition facts per serving and food exchanges are noted with each recipe.

Test Kitchen tips and sugar substitutes are listed after the recipe directions.

When ingredient choices appear, we use the first one to calculate the nutrition analysis.

Key to Abbreviations
CAL = calories
sat. fat = saturated fat
CHOL = cholesterol
CARB = carbohydrate
PRO = protein

Test Kitchen tip:
Handling hot chile peppers
Chile peppers can irritate skin and eyes. Wear gloves when working with them. If your bare hands do touch the peppers, wash your hands with soap and warm water.

RECIPE INDEX

METRIC INFORMATION

The charts on this page provide a guide for converting measurements from the U.S. customary system, which is used throughout this book, to the metric system.

Product Differences

Most of the ingredients called for in the recipes in this book are available in most countries. However, some are known by different names. Here are some common American ingredients and their possible counterparts:

* All-purpose flour is enriched, bleached or unbleached white household flour. When self-rising flour is used in place of all-purpose flour in a recipe that calls for leavening, omit the leavening agent (baking soda or baking powder) and salt.
* Baking soda is bicarbonate of soda.
* Cornstarch is cornflour.
* Golden raisins are sultanas.
* Light-color corn syrup is golden syrup.
* Powdered sugar is icing sugar.
* Sugar (white) is granulated, fine granulated, or castor sugar.
* Vanilla or vanilla extract is vanilla essence.

Volume and Weight

The United States traditionally uses cup measures for liquid and solid ingredients. The chart below shows the approximate imperial and metric equivalents. If you are accustomed to weighing solid ingredients, the following approximate equivalents will be helpful.

* 1 cup butter, castor sugar, or rice = 8 ounces = $\frac{1}{2}$ pound = 250 grams
* 1 cup flour = 4 ounces = $\frac{1}{4}$ pound = 125 grams
* 1 cup icing sugar = 5 ounces = 150 grams

Canadian and U.S. volume for a cup measure is 8 fluid ounces (237 ml), but the standard metric equivalent is 250 ml.

1 British imperial cup is 10 fluid ounces.

In Australia, 1 tablespoon equals 20 ml, and there are 4 teaspoons in the Australian tablespoon.

Spoon measures are used for smaller amounts of ingredients. Although the size of the tablespoon varies slightly in different countries, for practical purposes and for recipes in this book, a straight substitution is all that's necessary. Measurements made using cups or spoons always should be level unless stated otherwise.

Common Weight Range Replacements

Imperial / U.S.	Metric
$\frac{1}{2}$ ounce	15 g
1 ounce	25 g or 30 g
4 ounces ($\frac{1}{4}$ pound)	115 g or 125 g
8 ounces ($\frac{1}{2}$ pound)	225 g or 250 g
16 ounces (1 pound)	450 g or 500 g
$1\frac{1}{4}$ pounds	625 g
$1\frac{1}{2}$ pounds	750 g
2 pounds or $2\frac{1}{4}$ pounds	1,000 g or 1 Kg

Oven Temperature Equivalents

Fahrenheit Setting	Celsius Setting*	Gas Setting
300°F	150°C	Gas Mark 2 (very low)
325°F	160°C	Gas Mark 3 (low)
350°F	180°C	Gas Mark 4 (moderate)
375°F	190°C	Gas Mark 5 (moderate)
400°F	200°C	Gas Mark 6 (hot)
425°F	220°C	Gas Mark 7 (hot)
450°F	230°C	Gas Mark 8 (very hot)
475°F	240°C	Gas Mark 9 (very hot)
500°F	260°C	Gas Mark 10 (extremely hot)
Broil	Broil	Grill

Electric and gas ovens may be calibrated using celsius. However, for an electric oven, increase celsius setting 10 to 20 degrees when cooking above 160°C. For convection or forced air ovens (gas or electric), lower the temperature setting 25°F/10°C when cooking at all heat levels.

Baking Pan Sizes

Imperial / U.S.	Metric
9×1$\frac{1}{2}$-inch round cake pan	22- or 23×4-cm (1.5 L)
9×1$\frac{1}{2}$-inch pie plate	22- or 23×4-cm (1 L)
8×8×2-inch square cake pan	20×5-cm (2 L)
9×9×2-inch square cake pan	22- or 23×4.5-cm (2.5 L)
11×7×1$\frac{1}{2}$-inch baking pan	28×17×4-cm (2 L)
2-quart rectangular baking pan	30×19×4.5-cm (3 L)
13×9×2-inch baking pan	34×22×4.5-cm (3.5 L)
15×10×1-inch jelly roll pan	40×25×2-cm
9×5×3-inch loaf pan	23×13×8-cm (2 L)
2-quart casserole	2 L

U.S. / Standard Metric Equivalents

$\frac{1}{8}$ teaspoon	= 0.5 ml
$\frac{1}{4}$ teaspoon	= 1 ml
$\frac{1}{2}$ teaspoon	= 2 ml
1 teaspoon	= 5 ml
1 tablespoon	= 15 ml
2 tablespoons	= 25 ml
$\frac{1}{4}$ cup = 2 fluid ounces	= 50 ml
$\frac{1}{3}$ cup = 3 fluid ounces	= 75 ml
$\frac{1}{2}$ cup = 4 fluid ounces	= 125 ml
$\frac{2}{3}$ cup = 5 fluid ounces	= 150 ml
$\frac{3}{4}$ cup = 6 fluid ounces	= 175 ml
1 cup = 8 fluid ounces	= 250 ml
2 cups = 1 pint	= 500 ml
1 quart	= 1 litre